Autism

Titles in the Diseases and Disorders series include:

DISEASES & DISORDERS

Autism

Toney Allman

LUCENT BOOKS

A part of Gale, Cengage Learning

GALE
CENGAGE Learning

Detroit • New York • San Francisco • New Haven, Conn • Waterville, Maine • London

GALE
CENGAGE Learning™

LIBRARY OF CONGRESS CATALOGING-IN-PUBLICATION DATA

Allman, Toney.
  Autism / by Toney Allman.
    p. cm. -- (Diseases and disorders)
  Includes bibliographical references and index.
  ISBN 978-1-4205-0143-8 (hardcover)
  1. Autism--Juvenile literature. 2. Autism spectrum disorders--Juvenile literature. I. Title.
  RC553.A88A456 2009
  616.85'882--dc22
                                                        2009022640

Lucent Books
27500 Drake Rd.
Farmington Hills, MI 48331

ISBN-13: 978-1-4205-0143-8
ISBN-10: 1-4205-0143-7

Printed in the United States of America
2 3 4 5 6 7 13 12 11 10 09

Printed by Bang Printing, Brainerd, MN, 2nd Ptg., 12/2009

Table of Contents

"The Most Difficult Puzzles Ever Devised"

Charles Best, one of the pioneers in the search for a cure for diabetes, once explained what it is about medical research that intrigued him so. "It's not just the gratification of knowing one is helping people," he confided, "although that probably is a more heroic and selfless motivation. Those feelings may enter in, but truly, what I find best is the feeling of going toe to toe with nature, of trying to solve the most difficult puzzles ever devised. The answers are there somewhere, those keys that will solve the puzzle and make the patient well. But how will those keys be found?"

Since the dawn of civilization, nothing has so puzzled people—and often frightened them, as well—as the onset of illness in a body or mind that had seemed healthy before. A seizure, the inability of a heart to pump, the sudden deterioration of muscle tone in a small child—being unable to reverse such conditions or even to understand why they occur was unspeakably frustrating to healers. Even before there were names for such conditions, even before they were understood at all, each was a reminder of how complex the human body was, and how vulnerable.

While our grappling with understanding diseases has been frustrating at times, it has also provided some of humankind's most heroic accomplishments. Alexander Fleming's accidental discovery in 1928 of a mold that could be turned into penicillin has resulted in the saving of untold millions of lives. The isolation of the enzyme insulin has reversed what was once a death sentence for anyone with diabetes. There have been great strides in combating conditions for which there is not yet a cure, too. Medicines can help AIDS patients live longer, diagnostic tools such as mammography and ultrasounds can help doctors find tumors while they are treatable, and laser surgery techniques have made the most intricate, minute operations routine.

This "toe-to-toe" competition with diseases and disorders is even more remarkable when seen in a historical continuum. An astonishing amount of progress has been made in a very short time. Just two hundred years ago, the existence of germs as a cause of some diseases was unknown. In fact, it was less than 150 years ago that a British surgeon named Joseph Lister had difficulty persuading his fellow doctors that washing their hands before delivering a baby might increase the chances of a healthy delivery (especially if they had just attended to a diseased patient)!

Each book in Lucent's Diseases and Disorders series explores a disease or disorder and the knowledge that has been accumulated (or discarded) by doctors through the years. Each book also examines the tools used for pinpointing a diagnosis, as well as the various means that are used to treat or cure a disease. Finally, new ideas are presented—techniques or medicines that may be on the horizon.

Frustration and disappointment are still part of medicine, for not every disease or condition can be cured or prevented. But the limitations of knowledge are being pushed outward constantly; the "most difficult puzzles ever devised" are finding challengers every day.

Mysterious Autism

Autism is a developmental disorder that is usually obvious before a child reaches kindergarten. It is a confusing and baffling disorder that seems to strike little children for no reason and steals them away into a world of their own. Many such children stay locked in those worlds for a lifetime, unable to learn to relate to other people or to notice the real world. Even when these children do notice the world, they act as if it is painful or meaningless. These children slip away from their families into their own minds, but their parents and loved ones often feel desperate. Jonathan Shestack is the father of an autistic boy. He explains: "You want your child to get better so much that you literally become that desire. It is the prayer you utter on going to bed, the first thought upon waking, the mantra that floats into consciousness, bidden or unbidden, every ten minutes of every day of every year of your life. Make him whole, make him well, bring him back to us."[1]

For decades, doctors and other professionals believed that it was impossible to make autistic children well. Parents were told that their children were "hopeless" and that nothing could be done for them. As the children grew older and became adults, many ended up in institutions or cared for by their families throughout their lives. Today, however, this bleak picture is rapidly changing. Children with autism receive therapy and treatment from the time they are diagnosed. For some children the treatments are ineffective, but others respond remarkably well. Autism expert Deborah Fein says that up to 25 percent of autistic children can recover and be indistinguishable from typical people. Others remain autistic but learn enough skills to be able to relate to people and cope with the world as they grow older.

Before doctors had identified autism as a disorder, many autistic adults were put in institutions by family members.

Today's autistic young people are the first generation growing up with professionals and parents striving to make sure that they receive the attention, education, and treatment they need. The autism community is excited about the chance these children will have to live happy, productive lives and to be accepted by the larger society. At the same time, families and autism experts recognize that current knowledge and efforts are not enough. No one really knows what causes autism, how to best diagnose it, or which treatments work for which children. Certainly, no one knows how to prevent or cure it. The lack of knowledge is especially frustrating because autism seems to be an epidemic in many parts of the world. More and more children are being diagnosed with autism, while too little is being done to combat it. Geraldine Dawson, an autism expert and an officer of the organization Autism Speaks, says:

> As a science, autism research is just now becoming mature enough to yield what promises to be truly groundbreaking discoveries. With the increased awareness of autism, government officials and universities are now paying attention to autism, devoting more resources, and investing in state-of-the-art autism centers of excellence. President . . . Obama has expressed his commitment to improving the lives of individuals with autism through research and improved access to high quality services. Now, more than ever, *unified* support for research and advocacy efforts has the potential to yield real change in the lives of individuals with autism and their families.[2]

CHAPTER ONE

Faces of Autism

When Temple Grandin was two years old, she says, she was "like a little wild animal."[3] She arched, stiffened, and fought to get away when her mother tried to hold her. She was calm only when left alone and seemed to have no interest in people. Her mother feared she was deaf because she never responded to speech and never learned to speak any words of her own. She could sit alone for hours staring off into space. She also threw terrible temper tantrums during which she screamed and kicked in rage. If she was not staring or screaming, she might be rocking back and forth or spinning around and around on her toes. In many ways, she seemed unreachable.

Donna Williams, at age three, stared into nothingness, too. She remembers that she was almost hypnotized by the colorful "spots" (actually dust specks) that danced in the air. She was able to understand speech and to speak, but she could not have a conversation or share information. Williams had echolalia; she repeated what she heard instead of responding to the words appropriately. If her mother asked, for example, "What do you think you're doing?" little Donna would reply, "What do you think you're doing?" She also remembers that she heard only "gabble"[4] when people spoke to her. She resented the gabble and tried to ignore it. She preferred to be left alone and spin

11

An autistic child is often most comfortable in his or her own world, which may involve such activities as spinning in circles or simply staring into space.

in circles or listen to the sound that occurred when she repeatedly tapped her chin with her finger. She says she was comfortable only in her own world and did her best to tune out the real world.

Karen Siff Exkorn says her two-year-old Jake also seemed to be tuning out the world, but he had not always been that way. As he grew and developed from birth, he learned to respond to his parents like any baby. He could speak simple, single words and respond to his parents' conversation. He loved to give hugs and kisses and was a happy, playful little boy. Gradually, however, as he approached his second birthday, Jake began to change. He stopped talking and acted as if he were deaf. He stopped playing with his toys. Instead, he turned light switches on and off or repeatedly opened and shut doors. He would lie on the floor for hours, staring at nothing. He stiffened and resisted when his parents tried to hug him. He became clumsy and could not run or climb easily anymore. He threw terrible temper tantrums, especially when his parents could not figure out what he wanted. Jake's mother remembers, "He was drifting further and further away from us."[5]

Autism Is a Developmental Disorder

Jake, Donna, and Temple all have autism. In some ways they behaved differently from one another, but each manifested severe and similar developmental problems from an early age. Child development is the complex process of change that all human beings go through as they learn—from birth—to move, think, feel, and relate to other people. Developmental steps include thousands of changes such as learning to smile at a parent,

A Lost Little Boy

Christina Adams's little boy was diagnosed as autistic when he was three, even though he had developed normally for the first eighteen months of his life. She said, "Autism is a black hole, capable of crushing personality, reason and affection. . . . Slowly the signs became evident to us. Frustration or noise made my son bang his head or bite. He and I became a colorful pair, his head with its blue-yellow bruises, my arms purple with bite marks. His fear of vacuum cleaners changed to obsession. After the diagnosis, our bright little boy started walking in circles, flapping his hands like a broken-winged dove. Watching his small shoes trace a tightening O on the kitchen floor hurt more than his deepest bite."

Christina Adams, "More than Enough," *Los Angeles Times Magazine*, April 27, 2003. www.christinaadamswriter.com/writings_Los-Angeles-Times-Magazine.html.

learning to crawl, learning to walk, learning language, and learning to play games with other children. Within the first three years of life, even though they look the same as other children, the development of autistic children goes awry. Autism is often called a pervasive developmental disorder, because the developmental problems affect, or are spread across, so many areas of learning and relating. The term *autism* comes from the Greek word *autos*, which means "self." People with autism seem self-absorbed and have trouble responding to the world outside themselves.

The pervasive disorders of autism occur in three main areas of development. The U.S. National Institute of Neurological Disorders and Stroke (NINDS) explains, "Autistic children have difficulties with social interaction, problems with verbal and nonverbal communication, and repetitive behaviors or narrow, obsessive interests. These behaviors can range in impact from mild to disabling [because the severity of the autistic problems can vary, depending on the individual]."[6] Autistic children can be very different from one another, but all have problems in these three areas of learning and growing.

Social Problems

Social interaction is very difficult for autistic people. Some, such as Temple Grandin, seem to resist interacting with other people from birth. As infants, they struggle to get away when they are held. They may either stiffen or go limp when they are picked up. They do not look other people in the eye nor smile in response to a mother's face. Many do not like to be touched. While they are babies, autistic children may be quiet and passive or they may cry and scream for hours. Usually, however, they cannot be soothed by their parents, and they do not seem to enjoy physical or emotional contact. Other babies do respond to their parents and caregivers, but then withdraw from the contact sometime within the first three years of life. They seem to tune out the world and lose the ability to relate to the people around them.

As autistic children get older, they fail to meet typical social developmental milestones. They continue to avoid looking at other people's faces. Many seem more interested in objects

Autistic children can have difficulty interacting socially and may avoid eye contact and touch, even with their parents.

than in people. They do not learn how to play with other children. They do not know how to make friends. They may not hug and kiss their parents or hold hands with other children. They seem unaware of the social "rules" by which everyone gets along. Many seem to be badly frightened or overwhelmed when they are forced into social situations with other people.

A severely autistic child is often referred to as low functioning. A low-functioning child may have very little social interaction. For example, he or she may not imitate other people. If a parent tries to get the child to clap hands in a game or wave "good-bye," the child does not respond. The child does not point to interesting objects nor look at something when the parent points to it. The child may not notice when a parent or other child is sad and crying or outraged and yelling or excited or scared. Often, the child will ignore people and prefer to be alone. Many low-functioning children are attached to their parents and are upset when their parents are absent, but they do not know how to show their affection in any typical way.

A less severely autistic, or high-functioning, child may have different social problems. He or she is aware of and interested in other people but does not know how to interact with them or understand their behaviors. For example, the autistic child may try to join into the play of other children by grabbing toys or even hitting the other children. If he or she can talk, the communication may be overly honest and lacking in sensitivity. The child may criticize playmates' skills or tell the teacher that he or she is incorrectly organizing the class. Often, autistic children are unable to handle a group of people and will "melt down," throw tantrums, or run away, even though they want to fit in and be a part of the group.

Communication

The inability to socialize appropriately can be seen in communication problems of autism, too. Autistic people may have serious difficulty with verbal and nonverbal communication. Nonverbal communication is the body language, the gestures, and facial expressions that people use to relate to each other. Autistic children have a hard time learning what these gestures and expressions mean. Also, they may not use nonverbal signals correctly. Low-functioning children may not make eye contact, point to a cookie to communicate that they want one, nor nod and shake their heads for "yes" and "no." Higher-functioning children may learn basic nonverbal signals but be confused about others. If another person is upset, for example, the autistic child may either fail to notice it or respond by ignoring the person instead of with compassion or concern. If another child signals boredom or irritation by backing away or with a frustrated facial expression, the autistic child has difficulty picking up the signals. He or she cannot "read" the emotions of others and does not express emotions in a typical way. Other people may describe autistic facial expressions as "robotic" or "blank."

Many autistic children never develop normal verbal communication. According to Easter Seals, a national education and service organization, about 40 percent do not speak words at all. They seem deaf to the speech of others and may not even turn to the sound of their names. When they are babies, they do not babble, imitate words, nor smile at their parents. As they grow older, they do not respond to any spoken requests nor use speech to get something that they want. Others do learn to

Many autistic children are not verbally aware and may not respond to, or seem to notice, others speaking to them.

babble, smile, and even use words but then lose this ability, or regress. Like young Jake, they fail to develop further speech and stop using the words they learned as infants.

Other autistic children do learn to speak, but they do not always use words to communicate with others. Some, like Donna Williams, are echolalic. They may repeat exact phrases that are said to them. For instance, if a teacher asks, "Do you want a cookie?" the child responds, "Do you want a cookie?" The child may mean "yes" when he or she repeats the phrase, but may be repeating, or echoing, without meaning.

Children who do develop meaningful speech may also use echolalia to communicate. David Karasik was an autistic young man who did have language but often used speech in unusual ways. For example, if he became upset and wanted to leave a situation, he might say, "Luke! This old man, he played one! Come on, Luke!"[7] He did not know anyone named Luke. Perhaps it was one of the names he heard on a favorite television show. He was echoing pieces of language he had heard in the past, and using this language to get across his meaning: "Let's get out of here!"

Some high-functioning or mildly autistic people learn to use language in a sophisticated and normal way. Yet even they have verbal communication problems. For example, they may not know how to join in a conversation without interrupting. They may take words too literally and be unable to make sense of a statement such as "Chill out." To them, *chill* means a cold feeling, not "be calm." Autistic people also may sound artificial and stilted when they talk. Grandin, for example, was teased as a teenager and called "tape recorder" when she tried to talk to and make friends with her classmates. At the time, she could not understand what she was doing wrong. She says, "Now I realize that I must have sounded like a tape recorder when I repeated things verbatim [word-for-word] over and over."[8]

Repetitive Behavior and Narrow Interests

Grandin is one of the few autistic people who is able to explain her autistic thinking now that she has grown up. She has helped experts to understand a possible meaning for the third

problem area in autism—repetitive behavior and narrow interests. Repetitive behavior is behavior repeated over and over
again, often in an obsessive way. Actions such as spinning or
rocking are examples of repetitive, obsessive behaviors. Experts call them stereotyped behaviors because they seem to be
performed over and over, without purpose, and always in exactly the same way. Such stereotyped behaviors are also evident in an autistic child's play. Opening and closing doors and
repetitively turning lights on and off are other examples of this
behavior. More complex behaviors can be stereotypical, too.
For instance, an autistic child may insist on keeping to a rigid
routine throughout the day. The child may melt down and have
a tantrum if expected to eat breakfast before getting dressed if
he or she is used to the opposite routine. The child may have
to line up toys in a certain, very neat way before going to bed
each night. He or she may need to carry an object, such as a
piece of string, at all times.

Sensory Problems

Grandin suggests that stereotypical behavior is a way in which
the autistic person creates order in a chaotic world. She explains that autistic people do not process sensory information
in a typical way. Sensory information is the way people experience the world through vision, hearing, touch, smell, and taste.
In autistic people these senses may be either overstimulated or
understimulated. Stereotyped behaviors may be tactics either
to soothe overstimulation or to achieve stimulation when the
mind is starved of sensory information. Certainly, unusual sensory responses seem to be part of autistic disorders. Some severely autistic people seem not to notice the sights and sounds
around them. They may not even notice pain. Some will bang
their heads repeatedly against walls. Some will bite or scratch
their skin and injure themselves.

More commonly, autistic people are hypersensitive to stimulation. Grandin, for example, says she felt actual pain when
her hair was shampooed. She says, "It was as if the fingers rub-
bing my head had sewing thimbles on them." Even as an adult,
she wears her bras inside out because the stitching in them

Autistic Savants

A savant is a person with an extraordinary, unexplainable talent. About 10 percent of autistic people are also savants. Daniel Tammet is one of these people. He is shy, rarely looks people in the eye, cannot hold a job or drive a car, and finds grocery shopping too hard and overwhelming. At the same time, he speaks seven languages and is creating his own language. He is a mathematical genius and has been able to solve complex problems in his head since the age of three. Tammet explains that he sees numbers as colors, shapes, and mental images. He says, "When I multiply numbers together, I see two shapes. The image starts to change and evolve, and a third shape emerges. That's the answer. It's mental imagery. It's like maths without having to think.

. . . It isn't only an intellectual or aloof thing that I do. I really feel that there is an emotional attachment, a caring for numbers. I think this is a human thing—in the same way that a poet humanises a river or a tree through metaphor, my world gives me a sense of numbers as personal. It sounds silly, but numbers are my friends."

Quoted in Richard Johnson, "A Genius Explains," *Guardian*, February 12, 2005. www.guardian.co.uk/theguardian/2005/feb/12/weekend7.weekend2.

feels like pins pricking her skin. Loud noises also caused her pain. She describes them as "often feeling like a dentist's drill hitting a nerve."[9] Other autistic people have terrible problems with flickering fluorescent lights or brightly colored objects. Many feel as if they see and hear every detail in the environment and are unable to tune out distracting sights and sounds.

When she was a child, Williams had visual problems that prevented her from seeing wholes. She saw things, especially people's bodies, as individual, unrelated parts instead. For example, she would see a hand coming at her, then notice that the hand was connected to an arm, and then be startled to discover that the arm led to a head and a face. Other autistic people see and respond to details that typical people do not even notice. One autistic young man got focused on all the screws in the hallways of his school. He had to touch each screw in the walls as he went from classroom to classroom.

Additional Problems in Autism

Determining what most autistic people sense, experience, or understand can be difficult. The National Research Council's Committee on Educational Interventions for Children with Autism reports that about 50 percent of them are nonverbal or cannot communicate through language. They cannot explain how they feel. Many of them have problems with learning. According to the American Psychiatric Association, most children with autism are also diagnosed with some degree of mental retardation. No one knows, however, if this delay in learning is caused by autistic symptoms or if it is a true retardation. For example, Susan Rubin is an autistic woman who

An autistic boy receives auditory and visual stimulation in a learning exercise. Autistic people may have a hard time focusing and need multiple ways to keep them engaged.

was considered to be severely retarded until she was thirteen years old. At that time, she was introduced to a special keyboard on which she learned to communicate by typing. Even though she had never spoken, she did have language and was not retarded at all. Today, she is known to have above-average intelligence.

Autistic people may have serious medical problems, too. Seizures, or epilepsy, are common conditions associated with autism. According to the National Institutes of Mental Health, up to one-third of all people with autism have or will experience seizures during their lifetimes. Other medical problems can include severe allergies, digestive problems, depression, and anxiety attacks. Autistic people may also have attention-deficit/hyperactivity disorder (ADHD). They find it very difficult to sit still or focus on a specific activity.

Each One Different

Autism is not one easy-to-identify disorder. The word describes a whole range of disabilities that affect many areas of development to different degrees and may be accompanied by many difficulties. Today, experts and doctors define kinds of autism as a spectrum of related disorders that must be diagnosed and treated and may have a wide range of outcomes, depending on the individual.

CHAPTER TWO

Diagnosis on the Autism Spectrum

Autism is the catch-all term for what is properly referred to as autism spectrum disorder (commonly shortened to ASD). Currently five recognized pervasive developmental disorders are on the autism spectrum. All describe autistic impairment in the three main areas of socialization, communication, and repetitive behaviors and interests. The impairments vary in severity depending on which ASD is diagnosed.

No single symptom or medical test can determine whether someone is on the autism spectrum. Clinicians (doctors and other specialists who diagnose and care for patients and clients) observe behaviors and developmental difficulties in order to decide whether a child has an ASD. Usually, children can be diagnosed with ASDs by the age of three, and often they can be recognized even earlier. Early diagnosis is an important goal because the earlier an ASD is recognized, the earlier treatment can be started. The problem is that ASDs can be complex and confusing. Although the autistic warning signs and symptoms may be obvious, it can be difficult to determine exactly which spectrum disorder (if any) is the right diagnosis for a particular child.

The Diagnostic Manual

Typically, a medical doctor, psychiatrist, or psychologist diagnoses autism spectrum disorders. Diagnosis can be as much an

Autism spectrum disorder is typically diagnosed by a doctor, psychiatrist, or psychologist, who helps determine the best course of action for the individual.

art as a science because so many of the symptoms may appear in other disorders or may even be seen in normal children. Clinicians must use both their past experience with recognizing ASDs and the accepted standards of diagnosis in the professional community. In the United States, these standards and criteria are established by the American Psychiatric Association and published in the *Diagnostic and Statistical Manual of Mental Disorders, 4th Edition, Text Revision (DSM-IV-TR)*. (*"Mental"* refers to thoughts, feelings, and psychological development.) Each disorder on the autism spectrum has its own set of criteria that must be met before a diagnosis is made. Clinicians use the

DSM-IV-TR because it is agreed that the standards are the best tools available for recognizing and diagnosing disorders.

The five pervasive developmental disorders on the autism spectrum are autistic disorder, Rett's disorder, childhood disintegrative disorder, Asperger's syndrome, and pervasive developmental disorder–not otherwise specified (PDD-NOS). All are disorders that include autistic behaviors.

Autistic Disorder

Autistic disorder is sometimes called classical autism or Kanner's syndrome because it was first described and named by psychiatrist Leo Kanner in 1943. In the past, it was the only kind of autism recognized by experts. To be diagnosed with

Autism Epidemic

According to the U.S. Centers for Disease Control and Prevention (CDC), more children are being diagnosed with autism spectrum disorders than ever before. In 2007 the CDC reported that 1 in 150 children in the United States has an ASD. This translates to 560,000 people under the age of twenty-one. Altogether, the CDC estimates that 1.5 million Americans live with autism spectrum disorders. Yet autism used to be considered a rare disorder. Some experts say that the way autism is diagnosed has changed. For example, some people who used to be diagnosed as mentally retarded or odd, shy loners are now diagnosed with autism spectrum disorders. The diagnostic criteria allow many more people to be labeled as autistic than were in the past. Other experts doubt that changes in the definition of autism have led to the increase in autism diagnoses. They believe that the increase in ASDs is real. Some say that toxins in the environment or infections are triggering autism. In 2009 the University of California–Davis M.I.N.D. Institute reported that the reason for the rise in autism cannot be explained by changes in definition alone. However, they say, all the true causes of the increase are still unclear and need further study.

autistic disorder, a child must have autistic symptoms before he or she is three years old. At the time the child is diagnosed, a minimum of six autistic symptoms must be present, with at least two from the problem area of social interaction, and one each in communication problems and repetitive and stereotyped behaviors.

Examples of social disorder symptoms listed in *DSM-IV-TR* include "marked impairment in the use of multiple nonverbal behaviors such as eye-to-eye gaze, facial expression, body postures, and gestures to regulate social interaction" and "failure to develop peer relationships [friends] appropriate to developmental level." Some communication and behavioral problems are "delay in, or total lack of, the development of spoken language

Symptoms used to diagnose autistic disorder include avoiding eye contact (like this boy), repetitive motor actions, and delay in language development.

(not accompanied by an attempt to compensate through alternative modes of communication such as gesture or mime)" and "stereotyped and repetitive motor manners (e.g., hand or finger flapping or twisting, or complex whole-body movements)."[10]

Lee Tidmarsh and Fred R. Volkmar are psychiatrists and autism research scientists. They explain what a clinician sees in a child with an autistic disorder diagnosis:

> A typical example is a 3-year-old child who does not speak and does not respond when parents call his or her name. Such children seem to be in their own world when left alone; in day care, they tend to isolate themselves from the group. They do not play with toys but, instead, perhaps repetitively stack blocks or push a toy car back and forth while lying on the floor. They are sensitive to loud noises and cover their ears when trucks pass by. They flap their hands and turn their bodies in circles.[11]

Rett's Disorder

Rett's disorder may look like autistic disorder, but it is not. It almost always affects girls. Between the ages of five and thirty months, the baby's normal development stops. Tidmarsh and Volkmar explain:

> After a normal early infancy, the head circumference begins to [slow down in growth]. . . . Previously acquired fine motor skills [with the fingers, for example] are lost, and a characteristic hand-wringing movement appears. The lower limbs and trunk are also involved; affected girls develop a wide-based gait [when walking] and gradually lose gross motor function [movement of large muscles].

> . . . There is . . . a loss of language skills, interest in the environment, and social interaction; affected girls appear autistic. . . . Rett's Disorder is associated with severe mental retardation.[12]

The differences between Rett's disorder and autistic disorders are important; Rett's not only always includes mental retardation but also is caused by a gene mutation—a change in the inherited information in the body that leads to disease. Rett's is a very rare disorder.

Childhood Disintegrative Disorder

Childhood disintegrative disorder is another very rare form of autism. In this form, the child develops normally until he or she is at least two years old. The child has normal language, social interaction, and learning. Then, sometime before the age of ten, the child regresses or goes backward in development. He or she does not make friends with other children, stops responding emotionally to other people, and loses language skills. Behaviors and interests become stereotyped, and the child does not play make-believe games. Tidmarsh and Volkmar explain that the child looks autistic but often has a worse outcome than a child with autistic disorder. In other words, the chance of improvement is lower than for autistic disorder, and the child remains more seriously disabled.

Asperger's Disorder

Asperger's disorder, on the other hand, is the mild form of autism spectrum disorder. It is named for psychiatrist Hans Asperger, who first described the syndrome in 1943. Children with Asperger's have normal or gifted intelligence. Their language skills are not delayed, and they acquire other developmental skills at normal ages. However, these children do have trouble with social interactions and with repetitive and restricted interests and behaviors. *DSM-IV-TR* criteria require problems in at least two of the following social areas:

1. Marked impairment in the use of multiple nonverbal behaviors such as eye-to-eye gaze, facial expression, body postures, and gestures to regulate social interaction.

2. Failure to develop peer relationships appropriate to developmental level [unable to make friends].

3. A lack of spontaneous seeking to share enjoyment, interests, or achievements with other people (e.g., by a

lack of showing, bringing, or pointing out objects of interest to other people).

4. Lack of social or emotional reciprocity [give and take with other people].[13]

People with Asperger's, like this young girl, are high functioning but have a different view of the world than most people.

Children with Asperger's also may perform stereotyped behaviors and may depend on routines obsessively. Even though their language skills may be high, they do not know how to relate to other people; they do not understand the feelings and thoughts of other people. Tidmarsh and Volkmar explain:

> For example, conversational ability is hampered by intense interest in a topic (such as the solar system or information on video covers), about which affected children may speak incessantly. They may make socially inappropriate statements in public or, sounding like little professors, use unusual and sophisticated words.
>
> . . . These children can often complete high levels of education, but their functioning in adult life is severely compromised [hurt] by their lack of social ability.[14]

Despite these autistic problems, however, people with Asperger's disorder are almost always high functioning, so much so that they often cannot be diagnosed at a young age as can children with other spectrum disorders.

PDD-NOS

The last diagnosis on the autism spectrum is pervasive developmental disorder–not otherwise specified (PDD-NOS). This diagnosis is used for children with autistic traits who do not seem to fit into any of the other diagnoses. In some cases, it is used because the child is not as seriously autistic as a child with autistic disorder but is not as high functioning as a child with Asperger's disorder. At other times, it is chosen because the child does not have all the required symptoms for autistic disorder. Perhaps, for example, the child has language skills but is still severely impaired in social interactions and repetitive, stereotyped behaviors. *DSM-IV-TR* suggests that "this category includes 'atypical autism'" that does not "meet the criteria for Autistic Disorder."[15] Nevertheless, children with PDD-NOS are autistic and have an ASD. One psychiatrist once explained to a mother of a child diagnosed with PDD-NOS, "It's all the same. PDD-NOS is just a way of sugar-coating a diagno-

This boy has an autism spectrum disorder. PDD-NOS, a form of autism, may not be as severe as other forms of autism.

sis of autism. You can call it what you want, but your son has autism."[16]

Diagnosing ASD

If the diagnoses are "all the same," how do clinicians make an autism spectrum diagnosis? The rare ASDs are more clearly differentiated from the others, but Asperger's, autistic disorder, and PDD-NOS can be extremely difficult to tell apart, especially in young children. Many clinicians say that no difference exists between high-functioning autism and Asperger's disorder. Others say that autistic disorder and PDD-NOS are not meaningfully different from one another. Most autism experts, however, believe that *DSM-IV-TR* criteria are the best available at this time. They emphasize the term "autism spectrum disorder" in order to stress the common autistic problems that interfere with the child's development. They try to make their diagnoses less subjective and more scientific by using rating scales and assessment tests, as well as by carefully observing the child, interacting with the child, and interviewing the child's parents.

Listening to the Parents

Typically, a parent first notices that the child is not developing as expected and expresses concern to the child's regular doctor. If the pediatrician agrees with the parents, he or she will refer the child for an evaluation by a clinician with experience in diagnosing ASDs. Many pediatricians use a screening tool called the M-CHAT (Modified Checklist for Autism in Toddlers)

The first person to notice a child's autistic symptoms is usually a parent, who then voices his or her concern to a doctor.

to look for warning signs of ASDs. This checklist is a series of twenty-three questions for parents to answer, and can be used with children between sixteen and thirty months of age. The parent answers yes or no to questions about social skills, such as whether the baby enjoys games like peek-a-boo or riding on an adult's knee. Other questions ask about smiling at the parent's face, making eye contact, pointing at objects, and whether the child seems deaf or oversensitive to noise. And the checklist asks whether the child sometimes seems to stare at nothing or twiddles fingers in front of his or her face.

The pediatrician scores the checklist. If the child fails more than three questions, he or she may be at risk for developing an ASD. One problem with the M-CHAT is that it gives a lot of "false-positives." This means that many children who do not have an ASD fail the test. However, the psychologists who developed the checklist explain that "the threshold for failing . . . was set low to avoid as many misses as possible."[17] The goal is to be sure that a child at risk for developing an ASD is not overlooked. Therefore, the developers recommend that the doctor interview the parents about questions that were failed. For instance, if the parent answered "yes" that the child twiddles his or her fingers, the doctor would ask for specific examples or ask the parent to demonstrate the behavior. If the interview still suggests real developmental problems, the pediatrician refers the child to a specialist in diagnosing ASDs. At that point, a whole team of experts may be involved in the diagnosis.

Assessing the Likelihood of Autism

Once the child is referred, a clinician will interview the parents again. He or she will ask about the child's developmental milestones. The clinician also directly observes the child, looking for areas of delayed skills or unusual and autistic behaviors. Many clinicians use a rating scale such as, for example, CARS (the Childhood Autism Rating Scale). It can be used with children over two years old and rates the child in fifteen different areas of development and behavior—from relationships to people to nervousness to verbal communication to activity level to the clinician's general impression of the child. Each

Professor Eric Schopler

Eric Schopler of the University of North Carolina developed the CARS rating system for autism. He explains, "When I first came into the field, the diagnosis of autism could only be made by a highly specialized psychiatrist. . . . The diagnosis was both subjective [based on opinions, not on facts] and costly for parents. It was usually based on incorrect and inappropriate . . . assumptions [such as that it was caused by cold-hearted mothers]. We developed the Childhood Autism Rating Scale in the early 1970s in order to establish a diagnostic system that was based on observed behavior instead of assumptions, one that could be used reliably by any number of professionals, where the diagnosis was public and accountable.

The CARS used only 15 scales that can be compiled from direct observation, parents, reports, or clinic records. . . . I am pleased to report that it has been shown to have reliable . . . properties more consistently than any other scales currently available."

Eric Schopler, interview, "Ask the Experts: The *Advocate* Interviews," Teacch Autism Program, July/August 1994. www.teacch.com/schoplerinterview.html.

area is scored from 1 to 4, for normal, mild, moderate, and severe. For example, the child's ability to relate to people may look normal (1). The child may be mildly abnormal; he or she may be extremely shy or clingy with the parents or may avoid eye contact (2). The child may be aloof and unresponsive to the parent some of the time; the child has to be forced to pay attention to the parent and does not initiate contact (3). The child may be aloof and unresponsive most of the time, have no eye contact, and act as if the parent is not even there (4).

At the end of the assessment, the clinician adds up all the scores and gets a sum of autistic behaviors and their severity. Children who score below 30 points are judged nonautistic. Children who score above 30 are autistic, and scores above 36 suggest severe autism. Of course, in order to score a child accurately, the clinician has to know what is normal behavior for each age level and be familiar with autistic symptoms. He or she must be able to compare the test scores with the *DSM-IV-TR* criteria to decide upon a specific diagnosis. The younger the child, the more difficult this process is, if only because the child has fewer developmental skills to test. Even tests like CARS are therefore still subjective and dependent on the knowledge of the clinician. That is why experts say that no one test can be used to diagnose an ASD. The Centers for Disease Control and Prevention (CDC) warns, "Many tools have been designed to assess ASDs in young children, but no single tool should be used as the only basis for diagnosing autism."[18]

In addition to autism rating scales, clinicians have to get an overall picture of the child's development. A psychologist will test the child's intelligence and cognitive (thinking) skills. A hearing specialist has to rule out hearing loss if the child acts

A researcher assesses the social-emotional processing skills of a boy with autism by analyzing his responses to different facial expressions.

deaf. A speech and language therapist assesses the child's language development. A medical doctor may need to test for seizures. An occupational therapist determines how adept the child is at activities of daily living. For a young child this might mean toilet training, self-feeding, undressing, walking, playing, spoon-feeding, or using crayons.

The Importance of Correct Diagnosis

Even with the information from a team of specialists, it is difficult to diagnose specifically an ASD in a child under the age of three. A two-year-old child such as Exkorn's son Jake, for instance, can be diagnosed with autistic disorder by one clinician and with PDD-NOS by another. While the risk of autism may be obvious, the kind of autism and what it means for the child's development may be uncertain. Yet diagnosing ASDs early is extremely important. The New Hampshire Task Force on Autism reports, "There is agreement among physicians and other clinicians that children with autism spectrum disorder who receive treatment by the age of 24–36 months, have a better prognosis [projected outcome] than children whose treatment is postponed until later. For this reason it is critical that children be identified and referred for intervention as early as possible."[19] Some experts are experimenting with diagnostic tools that will allow clinicians to assess risk in babies by nine to twelve months of age.

Most autism experts agree that children are probably born with the risk of developing autism, so very early diagnosis does seem possible. Even if these experts succeed in identifying babies with autism, however, they will not know for sure why these children have autism in the first place nor will they truly be able to cure it. Clinicians concentrate on improving the diagnosis and treatment of autism, but other experts devote their efforts to understanding its cause. The cause may be just as complicated as the diagnosis.

CHAPTER THREE

What Causes ASDs?

For decades, many experts believed that autism was the parents' fault and blamed the disorder on "refrigerator mothers."[20] Since these mothers were not warm and loving, said the clinicians, the babies rejected the world and became autistic. Now, experts know this theory is completely wrong. ASDs are brain disorders, neurological conditions caused by differences in the way the brain is wired. These changes in the way the brain develops and works could be innate, or inborn. However, some scientists believe the environment may be involved, too. They suggest that innate sensitivities to something in the environment may adversely affect the brains of certain children and trigger the neurological changes that lead to autism.

This Is Your Brain on Autism

Grandin is not only autistic herself but as an adult has become an animal behavior expert and a recognized authority on autistic thinking. She uses an analogy to explain the differences between typical brains and brains affected by autism:

> The way I visualize it is that a normal brain is like a big corporate office building with telephones, faxes, e-mail, messengers, people walking around and talking—a big corporation has zillions of ways for messages to get from

one place to another. The autistic brain is like the same big corporate office building where the only way for anyone to talk to anyone else is by fax. There's no telephone, no e-mail, no messengers, and no people walking around and talking to each other. Just faxes. So a lot less stuff is getting through as a consequence, and everything starts to break down. Some messages get through okay; other messages get distorted when the fax misprints or the paper jams; other messages don't get through at all.[21]

White Matter Misconnections

As Grandin implies, the brain is an incredibly complex organ in which different areas communicate and interact with one another. White matter is the nerve fibers in the brain that link all the parts together—that enable the messages to get around. It is in the white matter, the wiring of the brain, that researchers have found variations and abnormalities that seem to go with ASDs. Sometimes the different regions seem underconnected—not enough fibers are connecting the different regions. At other times, parts are overconnected—many more connections are found in certain parts of the brain than is typical.

Psychologist Marcel Just of Carnegie Mellon University researches and compares autistic and normal brains at the Center for Excellence in Autism Research at the University of Pittsburgh. He has studied the brains of autistic adults who have language comprehension and normal intelligence. He explains:

> Our findings show that brain regions in high-functioning individuals with autism do not communicate with each other as effectively as those without autism, especially when they perform complex tasks such as . . . language comprehension. The results on language processing have also shown that individuals with high-functioning autism, when compared to those without autism, are more likely to rely on brain regions that process visualization, rather than communication. That means individuals with autism "think in pictures."[22]

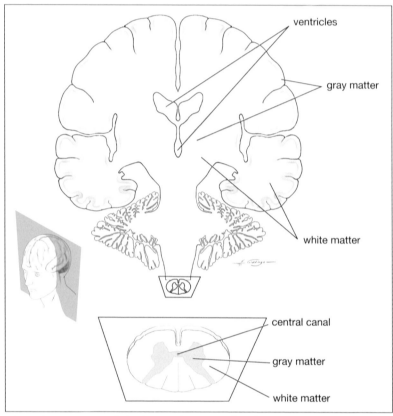

ventricles

gray matter

white matter

central canal

gray matter

white matter

The white matter of the brain, shown in this diagram, is the brain's wiring. Researchers have found abnormalities in the matter that may link to autism spectrum disorder.

Brain Functions

Scientists know that different areas of the brain are generally responsible for different activities. The cerebral cortex, also called gray matter, is the part of the brain responsible for higher functioning, such as language, thinking, reasoning, problem solving, voluntary movement, emotional responses, and perceiving the environment. It is the outer layer of the brain. The brain as a whole is divided into two halves, or hemispheres. Within the hemispheres are the four lobes.

The frontal lobes are at the very front of the brain. They are responsible for such activities as reasoning, speech, problem solving, and some emotional reactions. The occipital lobes are at the back of the brain. They are responsible for vision. The parietal lobes, just behind the frontal lobes, are responsible for perception of pressure, pain, touch, and temperature, as well as for visual thinking and imagination and coordinating input from the senses. The temporal lobes are underneath the frontal lobes. They are associated with hearing and memory. Deep within the temporal lobes is a structure named the amygdala. It acts as the brain's emotional emergency warning system. For example, it is responsible for the "fight-or-flight" response of the body that prepares the individual either to run away from a perceived danger or to get ready to fight. The amygdala plays a role in other emotions and in memory, too. All of these parts of the brain interact with one another or are wired to and communicate with each other through the white matter.

The lobes of the brain: the frontal (blue), the parietal (green), the temporal (purple), and the occipital (yellow). Different lobes of the brain are responsible for different activities.

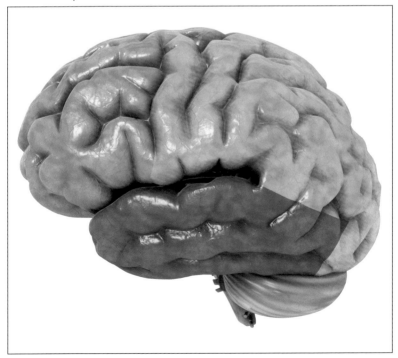

Mapping Brains

Scientists can map living brains and observe the activity in working brains by using brain scan techniques such as magnetic resonance imaging (MRI) and functional magnetic resonance imaging
(fMRI). An MRI is a medical test that uses a large magnet to cre-
ate a magnetic field around a person's head. Radio waves are sent
through the magnetic field. A computer reads the wave signals
and builds a detailed picture of the brain. With fMRI, scientists
can get an image of the blood flow in the area of the brain where
activity is occurring. They can watch the brain as people do specific tasks, such as solving math problems, looking at faces, or
reading. They can see the changes in blood flow that indicate
which part of the brain is being used to perform the tasks. They
can see how active that part of the brain becomes when it is required to perform those tasks. Scientists have used both techniques to compare the brains of people with ASDs to people with
typical brains. Their research has suggested several important
differences, although no one can be positive about whether the
differences are the cause of ASDs or the result.

Different Wiring, Different Thinking

MRI and other tests consistently show that children with ASDs
show excessive growth of the brain between ages two and four
years old. Much of this excess growth is in the frontal lobes. At the
same time, the nerve cells that make up the frontal lobes are
smaller than normal. No one is sure why this happens or what it
means, but psychiatrist Uta Frith, a renowned autism expert, suggests a theory. She explains that, from birth, normal brain development includes a "pruning process" that "eliminates faulty [white
matter] connections" and makes the brain connections function
more smoothly. Perhaps, Frith says, "Lack of pruning in autism
might therefore lead to an increase in brain size and be associated
with poor functioning of certain neural circuits [the wiring]."[23]

The wiring that lets the two halves of the brain interact with
each other is called the corpus callosum. In 2006 Just reported
discovering that the corpus callosum in some autistic brains
was smaller than in typical brains. He also found connection

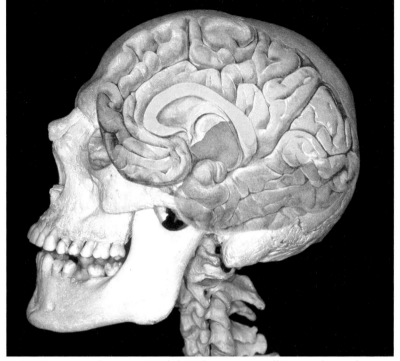
In 2006 a researcher reported that the corpus callosum, shown here in green, was smaller in autistic brains.

differences between the lobes of the brains of autistic and nonautistic people. Just did an experiment in which he asked people to read sentences and score them as true or false. He used fMRI techniques to see what happened in their brains while they worked on the task. The sentences were examples of low-imagery and high-imagery ideas. That is, some sentences were dry statements of facts. Others were statements that make people get a visual picture in their heads when they read the sentences. An example of a low-imagery sentence was, "Addition, subtraction, and multiplication are all math skills." One high-imagery sentence read, "The number eight, when rotated 90 degrees, looks like a pair of eyeglasses."[24]

When people with typical brains read low-imagery sentences, they used their frontal lobes to read and think about the statements. For high-imagery sentences, however, they needed to imagine or see the idea in their minds, and this activated first their frontal lobes and then areas in their parietal lobes. The connections between the lobes were made only when a visual image was needed to decide whether the sentence was true. Autistic people responded differently. Whether the sentences were low or high imagery, their parietal lobes were very active. Perhaps, say

Just and other scientists, autistic people depend on visual brain areas because the connections within the frontal lobes are faulty. Certainly Grandin agrees with this assessment. She says she "thinks in pictures." She explains, "Words are like a second language to me. I translate both spoken and written words into full-color movies, complete with sound, which run like a VCR tape in my head. When somebody speaks to me, his words are instantly translated into pictures."[25]

Fear Connections

People with ASDs seem to use different parts of the brain and use them in different ways than nonautistic people do. The parts of their brains that need to coordinate social skills and

Boys and Girls and Autism

Many more boys than girls are at risk for autism spectrum disorders. The ratio is generally believed to be 4:1—that is, for every girl diagnosed with an ASD, four boys are affected. No one is sure why this should be so. In 2009 British autism expert Simon Baron-Cohen suggested that hormones are the answer. At Cambridge University, Baron-Cohen studied the body chemical that gives boys their male characteristics—the hormone named testosterone. He and his research team measured testosterone in babies while they were fetuses growing in their mothers' wombs. They discovered that the higher the testosterone levels in the womb, the more likely the child was to have autistic traits in later life. Baron-Cohen says, "We've consistently found that the higher your level [of fetal testosterone], the worse your social skills and the slower your language development." He says this is true whether the baby is a boy or a girl. (All girls have some testosterone in their bodies.) Baron-Cohen says a child with autism has "an extreme male brain." Other scientists are skeptical and say more research is needed to see if Baron-Cohen is correct.

Quoted in Virginia Hughes, "High Fetal Testosterone Triggers Autism, British Group Says," Simons Foundation Autism Research Initiative, January 7, 2009. http://sfari .org/news/high-fetal-testosterone-triggers-autism-british-group-says.

emotional relationships do not connect and form networks in typical ways either. Some studies have shown that the amygdala, which is involved in emotional learning, fear, and sending messages to the frontal lobes, has fewer nerve cells in autistic brains. Scientists at the University of Wisconsin–Madison also found evidence that these atypical amygdalas in autistic children are hyperactive, or overaroused. The researchers tracked the eye movements of children looking at faces. They made maps of the brain activity that occurred with eye contact. The scientists discovered that the area of the amygdala that signals threats was very active when autistic children looked at faces, even when the faces were not threatening. Psychiatrist Richard Davidson, one of the researchers, says this perceived threat makes autistic children need to look away from faces. He adds, "Imagine walking through the world and interpreting every face that looks at you as a threat, even the face of your own mother."[26] An atypical amygdala may also explain why so many people with ASDs suffer with anxiety—their fight-or-flight response may be turned on too much of the time.

Faulty Social Brains

Social and emotional responses are controlled by several interconnected areas of the brain, particularly in the frontal and temporal lobes and the amygdala. Scientists theorize that these areas make up the social brain. Because of the social brain, babies are strongly attracted to faces and people; older children use language and play to interact with others; and everyone learns to relate to people and understand what others may be thinking and feeling. Many studies suggest that the social brain does not work well for people with ASDs because of a difference in wiring. Some studies have found less activity in the frontal lobes of people with ASDs when they are asked to describe social situations, such as whether two people are having an argument or enjoying each other's company. In 2007 neuropsychologist Robert Schultz used fMRI to show that the area of the brain that recognizes faces is underactive in young children with autism. Yet this same region strongly reacted when children were shown pictures of their favorite, restricted interests.

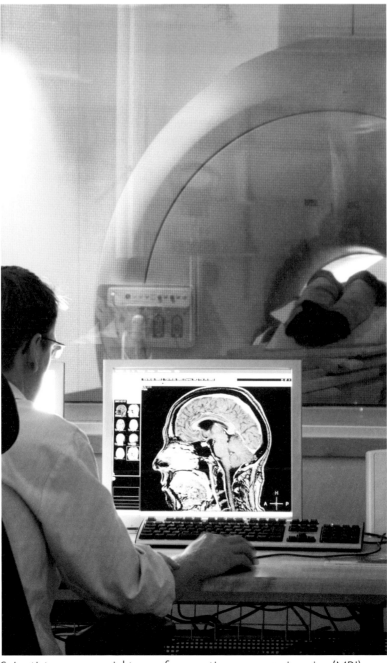

Scientists use a special type of magnetic resonance imaging (MRI) called functional magnetic imaging (fMRI) to study which areas of an autistic brain are active or underactive during various tasks.

Some studies find that different areas of the brain do not communicate smoothly when people with autism are making social judgments. Just asked autistic and nonautistic people to look at cartoons of different shapes and then explain what they were doing in a social way. For example, one triangle would push on another triangle and nudge it forward. The correct "answer" to this social situation was "persuading." Just used fMRI to measure which areas of the brain were used for the task. He was looking for how well the social areas of the brain were wired together and activated simultaneously. Autistic people had trouble with this task, and the different parts of their brains did not work together smoothly, as they did in nonautistic people. This was true even though the autistic people had normal intelligence. Just believes that this faulty communications network "is largely responsible for social challenges in autism."[27]

Genes and Brain Development

Understanding the neurological differences that exist with ASDs is important, but it does not explain how autistic brains came to be wired in an atypical way in the first place. Most autism experts believe that the answer lies in the genes. Genes are the packages of deoxyribonucleic acid (DNA) that code for how every living thing grows and develops. In human cells, genes are arranged into twenty-three pairs of chromosomes, with thousands of genes on each chromosome. Genes carry the coded instructions that determine how each individual looks, how the body develops, and how the brain functions. Variations and mistakes in genes often determine whether a person is born with a disease or disorder and what abilities or disabilities that person may possess. Scientists suspect that changes in multiple genes, somewhat like typographical errors, are responsible for ASDs. Finding these genes, however, is extremely difficult.

One way that researchers discover the role that genes play in autism is with identical twins. Identical twins have almost the same genes. Studies of identical twins with ASDs have shown that if one twin is autistic, the other is autistic up to 90 percent of the time. When a fraternal twin or sibling is autistic,

Studies have shown that if one identical twin is autistic, 90 percent of the time the other twin is also autistic.

however, the risk of autism is only about 3 percent. This strongly suggests that ASDs are genetically determined.

So far, scientists have found evidence that as many as thirty different genes may be involved in autism. For example, in 2008 researcher Christopher Walsh led a team of scientists at Children's Hospital Boston who discovered six genes that were faulty in a group of autistic children. All of these genes function together to code for building and strengthening the brain's wiring. Some of the DNA in each gene was missing or turned off. Other scientists have identified other genes that seem to be

Fragile X Syndrome

In about 6 percent of autistic children, the cause of their autism can be clearly identified. These children are autistic because of a change in one gene that codes for making a particular brain chemical. The gene is on the X chromosome. X and Y chromosomes determine sex. A female has two X chromosomes; a male has one X and one Y. A child inherits one of these chromosomes from the mother and one from the father. If one of these X's has the faulty gene, that gene may be so fragile (or likely to change its code even further) that the child who inherits it could be born with fragile X syndrome. Most of the time, but not always, a child with fragile X is mentally retarded. Up to a third of children with fragile X are also autistic or have some autistic symptoms. Scientists say that fragile X is the most common single-gene cause of autism.

faulty in some autistic people. However, no one has found genetic mistakes that are present in 100 percent of people with ASDs. This means, Walsh explains, that "we still don't understand the underlying genetics for more than half the kids with autism, so we have a long way to go to understand that, and to understand what non-genetic factors might also contribute. We know genetics is very important in autism, but we don't know whether it is the whole answer or not."[28]

The Environment and Brain Development

Many parents of autistic children are sure that genes are not the only cause of autism. They blame the environment, especially problems with allergies and vaccines. Little scientific evidence points to vaccines as the cause of autism, but many parents report that their babies became autistic after they were given vaccines. Some experts agree with them. Autism expert Bernard Rimland once argued that children could be born with a predisposition to autism. This would mean that the coding in some of their genes left their bodies unable to handle some toxins that do not harm other children. When they are exposed to these toxins, they become autistic. Rimland said:

> The genetic element seems [to be], on the basis of a good deal of evidence, that the children have a tremendously difficult time detoxifying heavy metals, including mercury. Many of the vaccines that these autistic kids have been given contain huge amounts, very, incredibly large amounts of extremely toxic [poisonous] mercury, which . . . was put in there as a preservative. And it's the genetic predisposition, plus the mercury, plus a huge number of increased vaccines that kids are getting which causes the increase [in autism]."[29]

Many parents and a few specialists feel that vaccines—especially the MMR (measles-mumps-rubella) vaccine—can trigger autism.

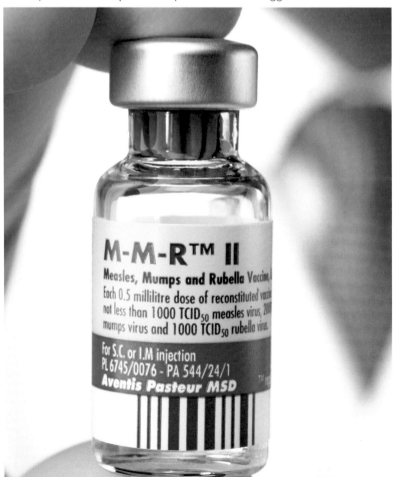

In other words, children whose genes make them very sensitive to mercury are poisoned by it, which affects their brain growth and makes them autistic. People who support this theory often believe that digestion problems and food allergies, perhaps triggered by environmental toxins or genetic sensitivities, also contribute to or cause autistic symptoms. After years of studies, the scientific community insists that vaccines do not cause autism. In addition, mercury was removed from vaccines in 1999. Nevertheless, many parents wonder if their children get too many vaccinations, even without the mercury, or if other, unknown toxins are combining with genetic predispositions to cause autism.

The connection between any kinds of toxins and autism has not been proved, but most experts agree that autism, which used to be a rare disorder, has become a common diagnosis in today's world. No one knows whether this has happened because autism is increasing or just because clinicians are getting better at diagnosing ASDs. However, the possibility that environmental toxins may trigger autism in sensitive children worries many people.

Both Genes and Environment Matter

Pinpointing the causes of autism is critically important to all autism experts because treating the disorder depends on understanding the cause. If Rimland was right about toxins, then special diets and other treatments to help detoxify the body are extremely important approaches. If autism is caused by genes that are partially turned off and fail to code for normal brain wiring, then treatment must concentrate on turning those genes back on. This is not as impossible as it seems. The faulty genes seem to be ones responsible for learning and reacting to the environment. Walsh explains that in young children, these genes could be activated, or turned on, by the right kinds of training, which could actually build new wiring and connections in the brain. He says, "Our work reinforces the importance of early intervention and behavioral therapy. The more we understand about genetics, the more we understand how important the environment is."[30]

CHAPTER FOUR

Treatments and Therapies

Autism is not curable, but it is treatable. Sometimes, people can even recover from ASDs and no longer demonstrate autistic symptoms. However, no one outgrows autism. Early treatment—the earlier the better—is the only way to lessen autistic symptoms and problems and to improve the lives and futures of children with autism. Experts may argue about which treatments are best, but everyone agrees that treatment, or intervention, must begin as soon as possible after diagnosis.

Early Treatment, but What Kind?

The Autism Society of America explains:

> Early intervention is defined as services delivered to children from birth to age 3, and research shows that it has a dramatic impact on reducing the symptoms of autism spectrum disorders. Studies in early childhood development have shown that the youngest brains are the most flexible. In autism, we see that intensive early intervention yields a tremendous amount of progress in children by the time they enter kindergarten.[31]

Without treatment, the prognosis (the predicted future) for children with autism is not very good. Most such children grow

Without treatment while they are young, autistic children may grow up unable to communicate or to be independent.

up unable to be independent and care for themselves. They cannot succeed in regular school. Many remain unable to communicate, unresponsive to other people, and unaware of how to behave in society. In the past, people with autism often ended up in institutions. Because they did not receive treatment as young children, they functioned at a very low level. Today, the prognosis for children with ASDs is much brighter. These children are treated intensively, with the goal of reducing or eliminating autistic problems that prevent normal functioning. For autistic children today, experts and parents have a great deal of hope, optimism, and high expectations for change.

There are a great number of treatments available for autism, but choosing the best treatment program for a child with an ASD can be difficult and confusing. Not only is each child different, but also many programs are unscientific and promise miracle cures to desperate parents. Yet parents are usually the ones who must choose a treatment for their child. This is hard because even the experts disagree about which treatment programs yield the best outcomes. Good treatments for ASDs are so new that scientific studies of their value are still ongoing. Catherine Lord, an autism expert at the University of Michigan–Ann Arbor, explains, "There is no one treatment that is going to work for all children or one treatment that is going to do everything for any given child over a long period of time."[32] Nevertheless, a few standard treatments are known to improve the skills and behaviors of most autistic children.

Applied Behavior Analysis

The treatment method backed by the best scientific evidence is called applied behavior analysis (ABA). ABA is a systematic, step-by-step approach to teaching specific behaviors and skills and reducing negative behaviors that interfere with learning and socializing. Desirable behaviors are rewarded, and undesirable ones are ignored. Records are kept of the child's progress, and, as each skill is learned, new, more complex skills are taught. The program concentrates on the specific behaviors that are disordered in children with ASDs —communication skills, social skills, and restricted, repetitive actions. Each skill is broken down into tiny steps that can be taught to the child and then shaped and molded into an appropriate behavior. The treatment relies on intense, repetitive training. Most children enrolled in ABA programs spend a minimum of twenty-five hours a week in therapy, both at home and in a clinic or therapist's office. Their daily schedules, indeed their whole lives, are devoted to treatment and, if all goes well, changing the wiring in their brains.

ABA is based on the idea that a young child's brain is very flexible and changeable. Scientists call this brain plasticity. It means that the brain can reorganize itself in response to learning and new experiences. It can develop new wirings and networks, and it can make up for a malfunctioning area by using other areas in its place. The environment teaches the brain to change and reorganize itself. Brain plasticity is at its peak in the first four or five years of life, when the brain is growing rapidly. That is why experts emphasize treatment for autistic children as early as possible. The first few years are the critical time when ABA therapy can do the most good. ABA therapists take advantage of early brain plasticity, says autism expert Geraldine Dawson, to "guide brain and behavioral development back to a normal pathway."[33]

ABA and Jake

Exkorn chose ABA therapy for two-year-old Jake. ABA therapists came to her house to work with Jake forty hours a week. Jake did not like his therapy at first. He often cried or had tantrums, but the therapists did not give up. Although the ultimate goal was to help Jake learn language and socialization, the first step was simply to teach him to sit in a chair and look at his therapist. Success built on success. Exkorn describes one part of this intense process:

> "Jake!" his ABA therapist would say encouragingly, holding up an M&M candy a few inches from her face to get his attention. . . . "Jake!" she'd repeat, drawing an invisible line between her eyes and his.
>
> No response.
>
> "Jake!" she'd say again, this time gently using her hands as blinders around his face to try to shift his gaze to her.
>
> Jake looked up at her.
>
> "Good boy! That's looking at me!" she'd say happily, as she put an M&M in his mouth.
>
> And then it all started again. "Jake!" I'd hear her repeat for a total of thirty times, before taking a play break to do a

puzzle or run around the room. . . . "Jake!" was repeated in every ABA session . . . until Jake learned to respond to his name. . . .

After thousands of hours of treatment over the course of a year, Jake slowly began to recreate sounds. . . . Isolated sounds became words that ultimately led to sentences. . . .

Then one day near his fourth birthday, as if by magic, Jake developed what experts call spontaneous language. . . . I took Jake out for ice cream. The man behind the counter . . . asked for our order. Just as I was about to answer, a little voice spoke.

"Nilla."

Jake said "Nilla." My son spoke his first word that had not been rehearsed hundreds of times in an ABA session. He had understood the man's question and answered him. All by himself.[34]

Applied behavior analysis (ABA) therapists work to help children with autism become more confident and interactive.

Rewired and Speaking

Jake's brain seemed to have learned from the weeks and months of constant repetition and intense practice. It had established new wiring for language. In the same sessions, Jake had learned to maintain eye contact, to accept and give hugs, and to stop having tantrums. By age four, he was on his way to recovery.

Many little children respond as well as Jake did to ABA therapy. Studies have demonstrated that between 75 and 95 percent of children with ASDs will speak by the age of five if they receive intense treatment such as ABA. Severely autistic children may not become completely verbal, but their autistic symptoms will lessen. Even learning to say and use a few words such as "mommy" or to like hugs and kisses can give these children a better, happier life.

DIR/Floortime

Since ABA does not help all autistic children recover, some parents choose other treatment methods, either along with or instead of ABA. One of these methods is DIR/Floortime. DIR stands for Developmental Individual Difference, Relationship

A father crouches on the floor near his autistic son. Floortime is a treatment method stressing that children feel more comfortable when adults interact with them at their own level.

Based. The name is meant to indicate that this treatment method does not emphasize teaching specific skills or behaviors. Instead, it stresses meeting each child on his or her level, understanding the child's feelings, and making emotional connections so that the child wants to learn. It tries to help the autistic child reach developmental milestones by connecting with the child and interacting in a nonthreatening way. "Floortime" reflects the idea that parents get down to the child's level, often sit on the floor with the child, and interact only in ways that are comfortable for the child. Crying and fighting, as Jake did at the beginning of his ABA therapy, is not acceptable.

DIR/Floortime was developed by psychiatrist and autism expert Stanley Greenspan, who established the Interdisciplinary Council on Developmental and Learning Disorders (ICDL). The method recognizes six developmental stages that children go through during the first few years of life. Typical children automatically meet these milestones, but autistic children need help. The ICDL Web site explains that the treatment is aimed at teaching parents to "follow the child's emotional interests" and understand "the importance of their emotional relationships with their child."[35]

Climbing the Developmental Ladder in Baby Steps

According to the theory, the first milestone for a baby is learning to cope with all the sensory information in the world. No matter how old an autistic child is, parents and Floortime therapists start here if the child is stuck at this level. The child may be oversensitive to stimulation or unresponsive to stimulation. If the child is oversensitive, the parents may be advised to touch him or her very gently, to speak quietly and slowly, and to try to help the child be calm. If the child is undersensitive, the parents may encourage interest in the world by talking loudly, swinging or tossing the child, and acting very excited.

The second milestone involves making eye contact and responding to a parent's voice. This is the beginning of love and attachment to parents. A child who has not accomplished this step may need to play gentle peek-a-boo games for hours so as to become comfortable with looking at faces. With older children, the parent may get down on the floor and join the child in an activity—even if it is just pushing a toy car back and forth. The parent plays beside the child and imitates the play. DIR/Floortime experts say that the parents have to "woo and entice"[36] the child to notice and enjoy their company.

The third stage is learning two-way communication. First, this communication is through gestures and sounds. The child learns that there is "power in his gestures." Parents and therapists teach this skill by reacting and responding to anything the child does. For example, if the child waves his or her arms, the parents ooh and ahh and wave their arms in response. The child learns that he or she "has the power to make things happen."[37] In the fourth stage, the communication grows more complex. The child is encouraged to learn more gestures and to understand the parents' gestures and noises. DIR/Floortime therapists say that this process makes a child feel safe and capable. It also helps the child to focus on the parents and pay attention to other people's behaviors and words.

Joining the Real World

The fifth developmental milestone involves play. Pretend play helps a child to understand emotions and to form ideas about the world. In order to feel accepted, an autistic child at this level needs patience and positive support for the stereotyped ways he or she plays with toys. In addition to praising and being interested in the child's play, the parents follow the child's lead and encourage curiosity. At the ICDL Web site, Floortime experts explain this stage with the example of Ryan, a two-and-a-half-year-old who was being taught to play with his father:

> Ryan noticed a flashlight. "What's this?" [Ryan] asked. Instead of grabbing it, his father responded, "Let's see if we can figure it out." He pointed to the switch. Ryan began pressing the switch, and after a couple of times the flashlight turned on. Ryan giggled. Then he shone it at his father, and his father made funny faces. Then they switched—Ryan's dad shone the light at Ryan, and Ryan made funny

faces. Through this little exchange both Ryan and his father laughed. Their exchange was warm and intimate, and for the first time, clearly pleasurable for Ryan.[38]

By praising a child's play and encouraging curiosity, parents and teachers can help autistic children better understand emotions.

The sixth and final milestone of development involves connecting play and the real world and developing logical thinking. ICDL describes this stage as becoming "rooted in reality." At age four, for example, Robbie might answer, "The moon is green,"[39] when asked what he had for lunch. In his treatment program, Robbie's parents sat on the floor to play with him. The ICDL Web site explains,

> Their goal was to prevent Robbie from withdrawing into himself and tuning them out. Each time he made a silly comment, they were to link that comment to reality by joining him in his play. . . . For instance, when Robbie slid a doll down the slide of the dollhouse and announced, "The doll is jumping out of the moon," his parents might say, "Where is the moon?" . . . as a means of joining his play.
>
> . . . Each time they joined him, they tried to help him tie his ideas to their ideas so that there would be a logical bridge between what he created and what someone outside him created.[40]

According to ICDL, DIR/Floortime helps many children with ASDs to make dramatic progress and relate to other people. It is popular with parents. Many professionals believe that DIR/Floortime is worth trying and makes sense as a theory. The proof that it works, however, is only anecdotal; that is, many examples are reported of children who improved. The therapists have kept careful records that document the children's behavioral progress, but, so far, no independent scientific studies back up these reports.

Alternative Treatments: Healing Sickness

Alternative treatments for ASDs have even less support in the scientific community than DIR/Floortime does. Nevertheless, these so-called alternative treatments are embraced by many parents. They and some professionals believe that autism can be healed with diet, nutrition, and medicines. Actress Jenny McCarthy, for example, says that her son Evan was autistic because he was physically sick. McCarthy is a powerful advocate

Is It Quack Therapy?

The Association for Science in Autism Treatment reports that many treatments for ASDs are not based on any evidence and are worthless. The warning signs of false, or pseudoscientific, treatments are:

1. High "success" rates are claimed.
2. Rapid effects are promised.
3. The therapy is said to be effective for many symptoms or disorders.
4. The "theory" behind the therapy contradicts objective [scientific] knowledge (and sometimes, common sense).
5. The therapy is said to be easy to administer, requiring little training. . . .
6. Other, proven treatments are said to be unnecessary, inferior, or harmful.
7. Promoters of the therapy are working outside their area of expertise.
8. Promoters benefit financially . . . [from] the therapy.
9. Testimonials, anecdotes, or personal accounts are offered in support of claims about the therapy's effectiveness, but little or no objective evidence is provided.
10. Catchy, emotionally appealing slogans are used in marketing the therapy.
11. Belief and faith are said to be necessary for the therapy to "work."
12. Skepticism and critical evaluation are said to make the therapy's effects evaporate.
13. Promoters resist objective evaluation . . . by others.
14. Negative findings from scientific studies are ignored or dismissed.
15. Critics and scientific investigators are often met with hostility, and are accused of persecuting the promoters [or] being "close-minded."

Association for Science in Autism Treatment (ASAT), "Pseudoscientific Therapies: Some Warning Signs." www.asatonline.org/resources/articles/evaluate.htm.

Actress Jenny McCarthy is a strong advocate for Defeat Autism Now!
She believes her son Evan's autism was healed through a better diet
and medical treatment.

for the organization Defeat Autism Now! (DAN!). She has written books and campaigned on television for the DAN! point of view. DAN! argues that the medical community is ignoring parent experiences and the overwhelming evidence that vaccines and other toxins cause autism and that medical treatments and diet can heal it.

McCarthy is just one of thousands of parents who say that their autistic children were born vulnerable to toxins. She argues, "Can we assume that some kids could be born perfectly healthy but vaccines then damage . . . [them], which could then trigger autism? Can we assume that some kids are more vulnerable to toxic overloads than are others? Can we assume that some children can't handle ALL thirty-six shots? You're [darn] right we should assume this."[41]

McCarthy says she healed Evan's autism. First, she put him on a casein-free/gluten-free diet. (Casein is a protein found in dairy products. Gluten is in wheat.) McCarthy believes that Evan's digestive system cannot process these foods because it was poisoned by his vaccinations. The careful diet, along with large doses of certain vitamins, lessened Evan's autistic symptoms. Evan had seizures and digestive problems along with his autism, so it made sense to McCarthy that "cleaning up the gut"[42] would help clean her child's brain. McCarthy used the diet, along with some other medical treatments, to make Evan well. By the time he was five years old, she reports, he no longer acted autistic. Today, he is a happy, typical boy.

Many parents use a special medical treatment, chelation therapy, to detoxify their children's bodies. This treatment involves injecting the child with chemicals that bind with metals such as mercury and remove them from the body. Other parents use hyperbaric oxygen therapy. It uses oxygen at high pressure in a chamber where the child lies. The idea is that pure oxygen can heal wounds and reduce inflammation in the body.

Too Many Success Stories to Ignore

Scientists continue to explain that vaccines, whether with mercury added or without, do not cause autism. The U.S. Institute of Medicine has stated that fears about autism and vaccines

Playing with Dolphins

Although scientists have no evidence that it helps, some parents choose animal therapy, such as swimming with dolphins, to treat their autistic children. In this therapy, a child is rewarded for good behaviors (such as imitating a spoken word) by being allowed to touch, kiss, or ride a dolphin. According to the theory, the child experiences positive emotions and learns to love animals and nature through this therapy. This increases the child's ability to respond emotionally to people. Other animal treatment methods use dogs, horses, or elephants, instead of dolphins. Therapists assume that the animals encourage autistic children to want to communicate and to be more social. Interacting with animals is fun and enjoyable, but experts say that research is needed to decide if these therapies really improve the functioning of people with ASDs.

are "not supported by clinical or experimental evidence."[43] Most scientists also argue that chelation therapy is dangerous and poisonous in itself. Others insist that treatments such as oxygen therapy do not lessen autistic behaviors in anyone. Nevertheless, thousands of parents say that they cannot argue with success. Diet and medical treatments worked to heal their autistic children. At least, says the Autism Society of America, more research needs to be done, and people need to be open to alternative treatments that may help autistic children.

CHAPTER FIVE

Living with an ASD

Most people with autism spectrum disorders are unable to tell the world what autism feels like and how it affects their lives. Even those who are high functioning, verbal, and intelligent often are unable to analyze their differences. Nonautistic people depend for understanding on just a few individuals who can explain and interpret the world of autism. They help everyone to understand autism's impact on the lives of those who are touched by it.

The Nonsensical, Terrifying World

Donna Williams is one gifted autistic adult who has the ability to explain the pain, fear, and confusion that her disorder can cause. As she grew out of infancy, she was able to make progress and learn, but it was a terrible ordeal because her development was not typical. She remembers her struggle to respond to the "real world" during her school years, when the only place she felt comfortable was in the world of "nothingness" in her own mind. She was aware that she was weird and different and afraid of being punished for it. Her teachers were sympathetic but thought she was mentally ill. Her mother called her "spastic"[44] and threatened to put her away in an institution. Other students taunted and rejected her. The young

---

Strangers Can Be Scary

Kamran Nazeer is a high-functioning autistic man who has over-come many of his autistic traits. Nevertheless, talking to people can still be frightening for him. He explains, "I feel confident and able, for the most part, to have conversations in formal settings —at work; when shopping in a store—there's an obvious point to most of these conversations. . . . I am also fine with friends and family, for I will see them again, and they know me already, so the consequences of failing in a particular conversation are slight. But talking to strangers is an undue risk. . . . Striking up conversa-tions with strangers is an autistic person's version of extreme sports."

Kamran Nazeer, *Send in the Idiots*. New York: Bloomsbury, 2006, p. 30.

Donna wanted to change in order to protect herself, but she could not. She recalls:

> As always, my motivation to interact [with other people] was to prove my sanity and avoid getting locked up in an institution. My inability to maintain this situation for any length of time was due to the state of mind of which "my world" consisted. In this hypnotic state, I could grasp the depth of the simplest of things; everything was reduced to colors, rhythms, and sensations. This state of mind held a comfort for me that I could find nowhere else to the same degree. . . . When I stayed aware and alert to what was hap-pening around me, it took a lot of energy and always felt like a battle. I suppose it appeared that way to others, too.
>
> If I was like this because of brain damage, it did not affect my intelligence, although it seemed that I lacked "com-mon sense." . . . Anything I took in had to be deciphered as though it had to pass through some sort of complicated checkpoint procedure. . . . It was a bit like when someone plays around with the volume switch on the TV.[45]

Donna's experiences as an autistic girl were made worse by the bad treatment she got from her family and the lack of therapy available to her while she was growing up. She was not even diagnosed with autism until she was an adult. For her, autism was accompanied by terror of an alien and unforgiving world. She knows that she cannot speak for all people with ASDs. She cannot say, for sure, that her own emotional experiences are the same experiences that other people have. Yet, fear and anxiety are reported by other people with ASDs, too. Williams believes she has seen the signs of it in the behaviors of other autistic children. Parents and experts often interpret the reactions of young children as forms of distress.

Without support from family and teachers, autistic children can grow up to be fractured and alone as adults.

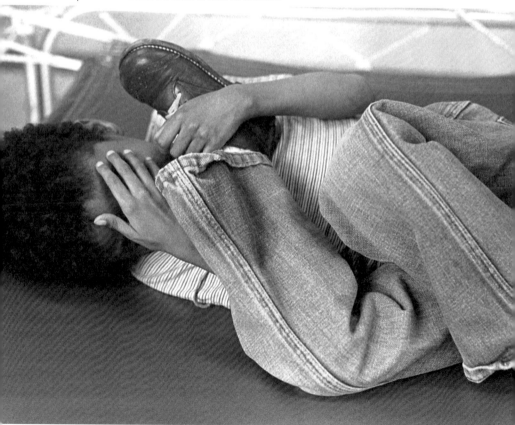

A Creative, Unique Solution

Temple Grandin had a very different family life from the one Williams endured. Her mother fought fiercely to understand and help her daughter. A favorite aunt was willing to do anything necessary to make Temple's life easier. The little girl developed, learned language, and was able to go to school. Yet Grandin, too, has described coping with a lot of fear and stress. She was not frightened of her family or teachers, but her autism left her in near-panic much of the time. When she reached adolescence, she began to have unbearable attacks of fear and anxiety. She believes that this distress is related to her sensory problems. She explains, "As far back as I can remember, I always hated to be hugged. I wanted to experience the good feeling of being hugged, but it was just too overwhelming. . . . Being touched triggered flight; it flipped my circuit breaker. I was overloaded and would have to escape, often by jerking away suddenly."[46]

While Grandin was still a young teenager, she visited her Aunt Ann on her ranch in Arizona. During the visit, she noticed the cattle being put, one at a time, into a squeeze chute so that they could be given vaccinations. Grandin explains, "A squeeze chute is an apparatus vets use to hold cattle still for their shots by squeezing them so tight they can't move. The squeeze chute looks like a big V made out of metal bars hinged together at the bottom." Immediately, the young girl was fascinated by what she saw. She had always loved animals, and she paid very close attention to the cattle's reactions. Many of them seemed to get very calm when the bars of the chute were squeezed together around their bodies. She says now, "The squeeze chute probably gives the cattle a feeling like the soothing sensation newborns have when they're swaddled, or scuba divers have underwater. They like it."[47]

At the time, Temple did not theorize about why the cattle relaxed, but she connected their calmness to her own needs. A few days after she watched the cattle in the chute, she had a terrible panic attack. It felt awful. At that time, she says, "My life was based on avoiding situations that might trigger an attack."[48] And she decided to try the chute that had helped the cattle calm down. She remembers:

> I asked Aunt Ann to press the squeeze sides against me and to close the head restraint bars around my neck. I hoped it would calm my anxiety. At first there were a few moments of sheer panic as I stiffened up and tried to pull away from the pressure, but I couldn't get away because my head was locked in. Five seconds later I felt a wave of relaxation, and about thirty minutes later I asked Aunt Ann to release me. For about an hour afterward I felt very calm and serene. My constant anxiety had diminished. This was the first time I ever really felt comfortable in my own skin.[49]

When her summer vacation ended, Temple returned to school and persuaded a teacher to help her build her own squeeze machine. She used it regularly and, over the years, has improved on its design. Today, decades later and despite the fact that she functions like a typical person in the world, she still uses her squeeze machine to help herself feel calm and in control. Other people may think Grandin's squeeze machine is bizarre, but for her it is one important way that she adjusts her autistic brain to the demands of the world of typical brains. Partly because of it, she has grown up to be a successful and talented expert in the field of animal behavior and has a rich and happy life. It does not matter if she does odd things or thinks in unusual ways. She knows that her brain works differently, but she says, "If I could snap my fingers and be nonautistic, I would not. Autism is part of what I am. . . . I have found my place along the great continuum."[50]

Coping Tricks Are Good

Another autistic person, Thomas A. McKean, has also learned to use tricks to keep himself functioning in society. McKean's life was more difficult than Grandin's in many ways. He was not diagnosed with autism until he was in the seventh grade and then was placed in an institution for three years. As an adult, he was also diagnosed with fibromyalgia, a disease that

Some autistic people wear a tight wristband, finding that the band's pressure helps to calm them.

causes chronic pain in the muscles of the body. This disease made all of his autistic sensory problems even harder to handle. Nevertheless, McKean is successful in the world as an author, a speaker, and an expert on the needs of autistic people. He travels frequently and lives independently.

One of the ways McKean learned to cope with his sensory problems is to wear tight wristbands so that the pressure can calm him. He has even made a pressure suit for himself to wear. It is a combined diver's wet suit plus a life jacket. McKean can blow air into the life jacket so as to increase the pressure when he needs it. He also carries a teething ring on his key chain and chews on it if he needs it to calm himself. "Get a life and get over it,"[51] he says. It is an autism thing.

The Daily Struggle

Despite his best efforts, however, McKean can become over-whelmed by the sights and sounds of the real world. He says that once, when he was at an autism conference, "I felt my entire sensory system begin to shut down."[52] He was frightened, but he was also determined to find a way to understand what was happening so that he could explain it to other people in the future. First, he grabbed the hand of another speaker sitting beside him. Then, he says,

> I watched with fascination as my clear vision faded to distortion. I watched as people became objects and shapes and clouds. I watched as the reds, blues and greens became different shades of gray. I listened as the volume on the universe slowly turned up. . . . Then my mind began to get fuzzy. I felt a tightness in my chest. It was hard to breathe and I felt and thought only one thing. "Get away. Get away. Not safe here. Go someplace safe where you will not be hurt." I looked down at my hand in hers [the other speaker's]. Something inside told me I was not to let go. I didn't let go.[53]

McKean's autistic experiences are sometimes terrible and painful. Despite the difficulties he faces, however, he, Grandin, and Williams are the lucky ones. They are so intelligent and high functioning that their autism does not stop them from "pretending to be normal,"[54] as McKean says. Most people with ASDs lead very different kinds of lives. Even when they are adults, almost half of all autistic people live with their parents. Kamran Nazeer, another well-functioning autistic adult, has written, "I am afraid that . . . there may be a hinterland of autistic experience, remote and underformed."[55] He means that their lives are so very far away from the normal world that they cannot reach out to it and that their voices cannot yet be heard or understood by the rest of society.

When "Normal" Is Not an Option

Sue Rubin, at least in some ways, is one of those autistic people. She is twenty-six years old and a college student, but she is almost completely nonverbal. She communicates with other people using a special keyboard on which she types her thoughts, using one, slow finger. She calls her disorder "awful autism." She is highly intelligent and yet cannot take care of herself in practical ways. She needs aides and caregivers twenty-four hours a day, not only to read her typed messages but also to take her to her classes and remind her to sit still and to focus on even simple tasks. Rubin finds eye contact very difficult. She carries plastic spoons with her almost all the time and twiddles and fondles them. They help her to calm down. She can spend hours "zoning out"[56] while she watches water flowing from a faucet and over her spoons. She is disabled in so many ways that she will never lead an independent life. The hardest part is that she knows it. She is fully aware that she is handicapped by her autism, and she is frustrated by her inability to change herself.

This strange mixture of ability and disability can make living with autism sad and difficult for whole families. Kim Peek was born with brain damage, including a missing corpus callosum. The neurological problems left him with serious autistic symptoms but also with amazing, geniuslike skills. He can remember more than 80 percent of everything he has ever read and reads two pages at a time—one page with each eye. He has memorized the zip codes for any town in America and knows thousands of historical dates—ask him the date of almost any obscure event and he will announce it, along with the day of the week it happened.

Yet Peek cannot take care of himself, is extremely shy, cannot look other people in the eye, and often mixes up words when he speaks. He has a happy and full life because of his father, Fran. Peek's father bathes him, dresses him, cuts his food, and puts the toothpaste on his toothbrush. Fran also accompanies his son around the world as he travels. Peek is a warm, loving, kindhearted man. He is admired by many people and is famous worldwide, both for his rare skills and because he was the model for Dustin Hoffman's title role in the movie *Rain Man*. Still, Peek's father worries. He wonders, after his own death, what will happen to his son and who will care for him. This is a worry for many families with severely autistic children.

Dustin Hoffman's role as an autistic man in the movie *Rain Man* was based on Kim Peek and Peek's own serious autistic symptoms.

Beloved Brother

Paul and Judy Karasik have some of the same worries about their autistic brother, David. They know he has the same feelings and needs as anyone else, even though he may not express those needs and feelings like typical people. They also know he needs protection from a world that is confusing to him. David loves being with his family, gives them kisses, and is happiest when he can act out his favorite television shows for them. As an adult, he went to live in a special group home where he could have some independence and get help with some of his autistic behaviors. Using a treatment method similar to ABA, the group home taught him skills of daily living and helped him to control his tantrums and meltdowns.

Then, after several years, things began to change for David. He came home for a visit acting stressed and anxious. When his family went to visit at the group home, he was in pain with an injured back. He broke a finger. Then, he had a broken rib. David never explained. Eventually the family found out that the home was under investigation. Residents had been physically and sexually abused by the staff. Sister Judy remembers,

Autistic Prison

Jonathan Shestack and Portia Iverson did not know what living with autism was like for their nonverbal son. They once wrote, "Our son Dov is now eleven. We watched with a mixture of joy and sadness as his eight-year-old sister surpassed him, and again as his six-year-old little brother has overtaken him and become his helper. I cannot even imagine what life is like for Dov—what he understands and what he doesn't. He is sweet and cheerful, but sometimes it seems as if Dov is in prison. And if you want to spend time with him, you have to get in that prison, too. You have to get very small and very slow and maybe—just maybe—for an instant you get to connect with him. Dov is so forgiving as we struggle to understand him. By example, he has taught us so much about patience . . . and the enduring power of love." (Since this passage was written, Dov has learned to communicate by slowly typing letters on a keyboard and has told his family that he does not like autism.)

Quoted in Karen Siff Exkorn, *The Autism SourceBook*. New York: HarperCollins, 2005, p. 273.

"I imagined David being hit, thrown down. . . . I imagined someone yelling at my brother. I imagined David frightened. . . .
David confused and hurt and scared and falling down. . . . And
no help. Nothing. . . . He was not able to tell us."[57]

Even when David was settled in a new group home where he
was happy, he would not discuss the abuse. All he would say is,
"I'd rather not talk about it." Paul and Judy deal with guilt that
they did not protect their brother and deep sorrow that he is so
vulnerable to cruelty just because he is different. Judy says,
"Why David was beaten . . . we will never know. We will never
know the circumstances. It doesn't really matter; David was
hurt. I don't know what's worse, violence or the fear of violence, but my brother had both."[58]

Toward a Better Autistic Life

Judy and Paul can only imagine what David went through and
grieve that their brother was not appreciated for his good qual-
ities. Theirs is a sadly common problem for families with autistic members. Almost all of the adult autistic people alive today

Many adult autistic people who grow up without early intervention
withdraw completely from society, lacking the ability to speak or to
interact with others.

grew up without early intervention or appropriate treatment. Many have no language; most live with their parents or in special homes; so many are unable to understand social interactions that they cannot protect or stand up for themselves. What about the children with ASDs who are growing up now? The hope of parents, professionals, and people with autism themselves is that their futures will be very different—that their differences will be tolerated and even valued by society and that their autism will not prevent them from leading full, independent lives.

CHAPTER SIX

The Search for a Cure

Autism spectrum disorders can be pervasively disabling. Parents of autistic children want to see their children cured and able to live normal lives. More than a thousand autism researchers around the world are looking for that cure. The goal of many scientists is to understand the exact cause of autism so as to prevent it in the first place. Others try to find a way to diagnose ASDs in early infancy so that the risk can be reversed with immediate treatment. Still others investigate treatment methods in order to determine the best way to eliminate or minimize autistic symptoms. The goal is a future without autism. Many people with high-functioning autism vigorously disagree with this goal. Like Grandin, they see autism as a central part of who they are and do not want to be cured. Instead, they say, the world should learn to accept and appreciate the autistic way of being.

Autism Speaks

Autism Speaks is the largest autism support group and fundraising organization in the United States. Its mission is to change the future for people with autism spectrum disorders. On its Web site it says, "We are dedicated to funding global biomedical research into the causes, prevention, treatments, and

Autism Speaks is the largest autism support group and fund-raising organization in the United States.

cure for autism; to raising public awareness about autism and its effects on individuals, families, and society; and to bringing hope to all who deal with the hardships of this disorder. We are committed to raising the funds necessary to support these goals."[59] In 2007, for example, Autism Speaks donated $30 million in research grants to scientific studies of the prevention, treatment, cause, and cure of ASDs. At the same time, the organization persuaded Congress to vote $162 million to fund autism research through the National Institutes of Health (NIH) and the Centers for Disease Control and Prevention (CDC).

The M.I.N.D. Institute Searches for Causes

The researchers at the University of California–Davis M.I.N.D. Institute share the goals of Autism Speaks and are partially funded by the organization. Because the scientists believe that autism is currently poorly defined and understood, they have begun the Autism Phenome Project (APP). (*Phenome* means "type.") APP is a long-term study of eighteen hundred autistic children begun in 2005. For eight years the researchers will evaluate these children and carefully record their symptoms, behaviors, diets, brain functioning, medical problems, and progress in learning. They will also examine the children's genes.

At the end of the study, the scientists will have a huge amount of information to compare among the autistic children. They hope to be able to answer questions such as why some autistic

Throughout the Autism Phenome Project researchers evaluate a variety of factors, including the diet of autistic children.

children have seizures, allergies, or stomach problems while others do not; how medical problems may change the prognosis for these children; why so many different combinations of symptoms are present in different autistic children; and why autistic disorders are in a range or spectrum in the first place. Even within the autism spectrum, these researchers believe that more subtypes of autism can be identified. The director of the study, David G. Amaral, says, "We have come to believe that autism is not a single disorder but rather a group of disorders—AutismS versus Autism. Each one of these autisms may have a different cause. We also think that each type of autism will most benefit from different types of treatment."[60]

In the future, accurate diagnosis of the subtypes of autism may point clearly to the best treatment method for each individual autistic child. The scientists at UC Davis hope to do more than develop new diagnostic categories. They want to pinpoint the causes of the autism subtypes, which will lead them to new treatment methods specific to each autistic subtype.

Along with M.I.N.D.'s Autism Phenome Project, Irva Hertz-Picciotto and Robin Hansen are conducting a study named

Vaccine Court

More than five thousand parents have filed formal complaints with the U.S. Court of Federal Claims, arguing that autism is caused by vaccines. The parents said that mercury in older vaccines or the measles-mumps-rubella vaccine (MMR) was responsible for the autism in their children. The court chose three of the MMR cases to review. On February 12, 2009, the court ruled against the parents and rejected the idea of an autism-vaccine link. The judges, called special masters, reviewed all the scientific arguments and listened to testimony from medical experts. The special masters ruled that the parents had failed to demonstrate any evidence of their claims that the MMR vaccine caused autism in their children. Lawyers for the parents are considering appealing the decision.

Childhood Autism Risks from Genetics and the Environment (CHARGE). The scientists not only look for changes in the genes of autistic children; they also look for such factors as any toxins in their environments, whether their mothers were exposed to toxins during pregnancy, what sicknesses the child has, and which foods the child first ate. They look for medical or biological problems that may affect brain development. They measure fats in the blood such as cholesterol, check how the children's immune systems work, and examine the brain chemicals that affect the brain's wiring. If, for example, CHARGE and APP scientists discover a missing chemical in the brains of one subtype of autistic children, they may be able to treat the autism with a medicine that replaces the chemical. If they discover a toxin that leads to another autism subtype, they could prevent it altogether by warning families to avoid that toxin, especially while the mother is pregnant.

Attacked Before Birth?

In 2008 the researchers at the M.I.N.D. Institute reported that they had found a significant abnormality in the immune systems of some mothers who gave birth to autistic children. The immune system is the body's complex method of protecting itself from diseases and foreign invaders, such as germs. When the immune system has successfully fought off an invader, it produces antibodies that can be found in the blood. Sometimes the immune system goes awry and attacks something that is not foreign. This can cause diseases in which the body seems to attack itself. In the case of the mothers of autistic children, the immune system seemed to have attacked the baby as it was growing within the mother. The antibodies seemed to be reactions to a protein in the growing babies' brains. At the same time, scientists at Harvard University discovered the same antibodies in mothers they were studying. What these antibodies do and why they formed is still a mystery to the scientists. However, they did discover that the children had a particular kind of autism. They seemed to develop normally after birth and then regress. Perhaps these children represent one subtype of the cause of autism.

Identifying the antibodies is important because they can be found in a simple blood test. That means that some children at risk for autism could someday be diagnosed at birth. Many scientists believe that treating children in the first year of life could stop autism in its tracks. Of course, the blood test would work only for those children within this particular autism subtype, but the scientists are excited to have already found evidence of one autism marker.

Baby Behavior for Diagnosis

Sally Ozonoff, of the M.I.N.D. Institute, is looking for other kinds of autism markers. She is trying to identify behaviors in the first year of life that can diagnose autism risk. She explains, "Behavioral science over the last 40 years has provided very reliable indicators of autism starting at age 2 or 3. We are determining the behavioral indicators to reliably diagnose autism earlier—maybe even as early as 12 months of age."[61]

In 2008 Ozonoff reported that twelve-month-old babies could already show symptoms of autism. She studied sixty-six babies born to families who already had one child diagnosed with an ASD. She chose these children because autism can run in families. She predicted that at least some of these babies would develop autism later in life. Ozonoff gave all the babies simple toys to play with and videotaped their responses. Nine of these babies did develop autism by the time they were three years old, and seven of them had played with their toys in a very repetitive way. They spun and rotated the toys. They also did things like look at the toys out of the corners of their eyes or stare intently at them for a long time. These behaviors almost never occurred in the babies who did not develop autism. Ozonoff says, "We wanted to directly test whether or not repetitive behaviors so characteristic of autism might actually be apparent earlier and therefore useful in early diagnosis. . . . Our results suggest that these particular behaviors might be useful to include in screening tests."[62]

If scientists such as Ozonoff succeed, ASDs may someday be routinely diagnosed in the first year of life. Parents and pediatricians could be taught what signs to be alert for in developing infants. Easy, early diagnosis could make early intervention easy,

In one study, several of the babies later diagnosed with autism played with their toys in a very repetitive way. Observing such repetitive behaviors in babies may serve as a tool for early diagnosis of the disorder.

too. However, it still would not tell parents and clinicians which treatment is best.

Medicines for Treating Autism

The research of some scientists suggests that the treatments of the future may be medicines and drug therapies. For example, Andrew Zimmerman of the Kennedy Krieger Institute in Baltimore, Maryland, studied the brains of autistic people after their deaths. He and his team discovered that the brains were often irritated and inflamed and that they had high levels of certain proteins that do not occur in typical brains. In 2006 another Kennedy Krieger researcher, Elaine Tierney, found very low levels of cholesterol in a small subgroup of autistic children. She says that this finding suggests their bodies have a limited ability to make cholesterol. And cholesterol is especially necessary to brain functioning.

At the University of California–Los Angeles, Alcino Silva and his research team tested a drug named rapamycin on laboratory mice that had a kind of rare disease that also occurs in people. The disease is called tuberous sclerosis complex and is caused by a malfunctioning gene. It causes mental retardation, and more than half the people with this disease are also autistic. The mice given rapamycin improved dramatically in their ability to learn and remember mazes. In 2008 Silva remarked, "This is the first study to demonstrate that the drug rapamycin can repair learning deficits related to a genetic mutation that causes autism in humans. The same mutation in animals produces learning disorders, which we were able to eliminate in adult mice."[63] Perhaps someday drug treatments like this will be available for the chemical problems that appear in subtypes of autism in people, as well.

Toward Evidence of What Works

Research on the current treatment methods that are used with autistic children is also ongoing. At the University of Rochester in Rochester, New York, Susan Hyman is studying the effects of a gluten-free/casein-free diet on children with ASDs. She says that about 50 percent of the preschool children with ASDs in the Rochester area are put on these diets by their parents. No scientific research has ever shown that these diets are help-ful, so Hyman wants to test the diet's value. She says:

> We have . . . evidence that many children with autism are at nutritional risk because of their self-imposed dietary re-strictions [their refusal to eat many foods], and that . . . the [gluten-free/casein-free] diet may result in greater risk. Thus, it is critical to determine whether the diet has beneficial effects on some patients and to develop criteria for identification of children whose behavior may im-prove with dietary intervention.[64]

Researchers are looking at the types and severity of autistic symptoms, their goal being the ability to predict which children will benefit from ABA therapy.

Another researcher at the University of Rochester, Rafael Klorman, wants to find out why some children do not improve with ABA treatment. In his study he will examine the genes of a group of children in ABA therapy to look for differences among them. He will also look at the severity of every child's autistic symptoms and the kinds of symptoms they have. Perhaps some symptoms, such as spinning in circles, indicate children who do not respond to the treatment method. He hopes that someday he and other experts will be able to predict which children will benefit from ABA therapy and which need different treatments.

Studies such as these are very important so that, in the future, treatments can be tailored to meet the specific needs of every child. Autism Speaks explains, "Currently there are no commonly accepted standards for autism treatment, and families are often left to navigate the course of their child's future on their own. . . . We believe that all families should have access to state-of-the-art care."[65]

Rejecting All Cures

Some people with high-functioning autism vigorously object to the treatment goals of researchers and groups such as Autism Speaks. Michelle Dawson, for example, is an autistic woman who argues that autistic brains may be different from typical

Some autistic people feel strongly that they should be accepted as they are and not "cured." They live full, happy lives as autistic adults.

brains, but they are not inferior. She says autistic thinking should be treated with respect. Autistics.org is a Web community of autistic people who agree that the world is prejudiced against autism. They are one of many activist organizations who argue that autism is just another way of thinking and feeling. They say that their differences should be accepted and understood, not treated or cured. Autistics.org calls itself "The Real Voice of Autism."[66]

Jim Sinclair, a member of Autistics.org, does not wish to be nonautistic. He says:

> Autism is a way of being. It is not possible to separate the person from the autism. Therefore, when parents say, "I wish my child did not have autism," what they're really saying is, "I wish the autistic child I have did not exist, and I had a different (non-autistic) child instead."

> Read that again. This is what we hear when you mourn over our existence. This is what we hear when you pray for a cure. This is what we know, when you tell us of your fondest hopes and dreams for us: that your greatest wish is that one day we will cease to be, and strangers you can love will move in behind our faces.[67]

Amanda Baggs, another poster at Autistics.org, agrees with Sinclair. She says that she wants to change society, not herself. She does not want to "act more normal." She wants society to value her as a person. Just because, for example, she writes better than she speaks, she does not want her difficulties to be seen as "defects." She knows that she is different, but she does not want autism to be "eliminated," prevented, or cured. She explains:

> I . . . know what it's like to not have a job or attend conventional school, to need a substantial amount of assistance in day-to-day life, to not be married, to not relate well to people, to have a decreased sense of danger, to not be able to talk, and so on. But these things, although they are quoted as being the source of pain to many parents, are much less of a source of pain to me, and most of my

pain in this respect is much more based in society—its prejudices and its unwillingness to accommodate people like me—than in autism. Even many of my intrinsic difficulties as an autistic person could fade into the background given the proper societal setting. Any pain that is related in some way to autism, I would still take any day compared to the idea of not being autistic. I like what I am, in all of its flawless imperfection.[68]

Just a Coffee Shop

Chandima Rajapatirana is a severely autistic man who lives in Sri Lanka. He learned to communicate by typing on a keyboard when he was seventeen years old. He and his mother want to help the autistic people in his country live happier lives. His goal for the future is a simple one. He wants to open a coffee shop. He explains:

A coffee house where people with and without disabilities can work together is perhaps our most ambitious project. Employment is not only essential for our self esteem it is also necessary to establish us as full members of society. Our coffee house will provide employment as well as open mike nights showcasing talent and space for artists to display their creations.

Such a place will provide the ideal environment for our often-separate worlds to mingle, and learn to respect and like each other.

Eating marvelous meals, sipping a refreshing cup, listening to wonderful poetry or music, surrounded by beautiful paintings, we will relax, and learn to build an integrated community.

Chandima Rajapatirana, "Coffee/Tea House Project," EASE. http://eassrilanka .org/coffee.html.

Who Is Right?

Perhaps activists such as Baggs and Sinclair are right that autism has value. Perhaps the unique autistic way of thinking contributes to society. Grandin, for example, believes that she understands animal behavior so well because of her autistic way of thinking. Nevertheless, she is grateful for her mother's efforts to help her learn and adjust to society. Nazeer, a highly successful writer and government policy adviser, supposes that his superior intelligence is somehow related to his autism. He believes, however, that he is able to use that intelligence in the real world only because of the professional treatment he got as a child. He explains, "I feel empowered, but there's no cause to disregard the reasons for my empowerment."[69]

Exkorn says maybe both sides in the argument are correct. She thinks that autistic people can be both respected and treated for autism. She says:

> Everyone should be respected and appreciated for his or her uniqueness. . . . Treatment is not the enemy. Treatment for autism can be seen as the equivalent of schooling for the typical child. Both can help children achieve their full potential by identifying and nurturing core strengths and individual differences. Why shouldn't children with autism have the same opportunities to learn and grow as typical children?[70]

Growing and reaching their full potential are truly the futures that everyone wants for people with autism.

Notes

Introduction: Mysterious Autism

1. Quoted in Karen Siff Exkorn, *The Autism Sourcebook: Everything You Need to Know About Diagnosis, Treatment, Coping, and Healing.* New York: HarperCollins, 2005, p. 181.
2. Geraldine Dawson, "2008 Autism Science Achievements," Autism Speaks: Science News, January 8, 2009. www .autismspeaks.org/science/science_news/dawson_year_in_ science_2008.php.

Chapter One: Faces of Autism

3. Temple Grandin, *Thinking in Pictures: And Other Reports from My Life with Autism.* New York: Doubleday, 1995, p. 43.
4. Donna Williams, *Nobody Nowhere: The Extraordinary Autobiography of an Autistic.* New York: Avon, 1992, pp. 3–4.
5. Exkorn, *The Autism Sourcebook*, p. 2.
6. National Institute of Neurological Disorders and Stroke, National Institutes of Health, "Autism Fact Sheet," October 2008. www.ninds.nih.gov/disorders/autism/detail_autism. htm.
7. Quoted in Paul Karasik and Judy Karasik, *The Ride Together: A Brother and Sister's Memoir of Autism in the Family.* New York: Washington Square, 2003, p. 115.
8. Grandin, *Thinking in Pictures*, pp. 33–34.
9. Grandin, *Thinking in Pictures*, pp. 66–67.

Chapter Two: Diagnosis on the Autism Spectrum

10. Quoted in Centers for Disease Control and Prevention (CDC), "*DSM IV-TR* Diagnostic Criteria for the Pervasive Developmental Disorders," July 3, 2007. www.cdc.gov/ncbd dd/autism/overview_diagnostic_criteria.htm.

11. Lee Tidmarsh and Fred R. Volkmar, "Diagnosis and Epidemiology of Autism Spectrum Disorders," *Canadian Journal of Psychiatry*, vol. 48, no. 8, September 2003, p. 518. ww1.cpa-apc.org:8080/Publications/Archives/CJP/2003 /september/tidmarsh.asp.
12. Tidmarsh and Volkmar, "Diagnosis and Epidemiology of Autism Spectrum Disorders," pp. 518–19.
13. Quoted in CDC, "*DSM IV-TR* Diagnostic Criteria for the Pervasive Developmental Disorders."
14. Tidmarsh and Volkmar, "Diagnosis and Epidemiology of Autism Spectrum Disorders," p. 519.
15. Quoted in CDC, "*DSM IV-TR* Diagnostic Criteria for the Pervasive Developmental Disorders."
16. Quoted in Exkorn, *The Autism Sourcebook*, p. 27.
17. Jamie M. Kleinman et al., "The Modified Checklist for Autism in Toddlers: A Followup Study Investigating the Early Detection of Autism Spectrum Disorders," *Journal of Autism and Developmental Disorders*, vol. 38, 2008, pp. 827–39.
18. CDC, "Autism Information Center: Screening and Diagnosis," February 7, 2007. www.cdc.gov/ncbddd/autism/screen ing.htm.
19. New Hampshire Task Force on Autism, "Part One: Assessment and Interventions," p. 13. http://iod.unh.edu/atf.pdf.

Chapter Three: What Causes ASDs?

20. Quoted in Exkorn, *The Autism Sourcebook*, p. 75.
21. Temple Grandin and Catherine Johnson, *Animals in Translation: Using the Mysteries of Autism to Decode Animal Behavior*. New York: Scribner, 2005, pp. 89–90.
22. Marcel Just, "Project III: Systems Connectivity and Brain Activation: Imaging Studies of Language and Perception," Center for Excellence in Autism Research. www.wpic.pitt .edu/research/CeFAR/research/Roj%20III%20Just.htm.
23. Uta Frith and Elisabeth Hill, *Autism: Mind and Brain*. New York: Oxford University Press, 2004, p. 5.
24. Quoted in AutismConnect News, "Ground-Breaking Studies Discover Brain Differences in Autism," December 7,

2006. www.autismconnect.org/news.asp?section=00010001 &itemtype=news&id=5816.

25. Grandin, *Thinking in Pictures*, p. 19.

26. Quoted in Paroma Basu, "Study: Eye Contact Triggers Threat Signals in Autistic Children's Brains," *University of Wisconsin–Madison News*, March 7, 2005. www.news.wisc .edu/10772.

27. Quoted in *e! Science News*, "Autism's Social Struggles Due to Disrupted Communication Networks in Brain," July 23, 2008. http://esciencenews.com/articles/2008/07/23/autisms .social.struggles.due.disrupted.communication.networks .brain.

28. Quoted in Daniel J. DeNoon, "Autism Cause: Brain Development Genes?" WebMD Health News, July 10, 2008. www .webmd.com/brain/autism/news/20080710/autism-cause-brain-development-genes.

29. Bernard Rimland, interview by Paula Zahn, "Vaccines Contributing to Rise in Autism?" CNN, transcript, November 20, 2002, reprinted at the Autism Research Institute. www.autism .com/ triggers/vaccine/cnntranscript.htm.

30. Quoted in Nikhil Swaminathan, "Autism Genes That Control Early Learning," *Scientific American*, July 11, 2008. www.sciam.com/article.cfm?id=autism-genes-that-control.

Chapter Four: Treatments and Therapies

31. Autism Society of America, "Autism FAQ," www.autism-so ciety.org/site/PageServer?pagename=about_FAQ.

32. Quoted in Jane Weaver, "Inside the Autism Treatment Maze," MSNBC.com, August 9, 2005. www.msnbc.msn .com/id/6948119.

33. Quoted in Teresa J. Foden and Connie Anderson, "Social Skills Interventions: Getting to the Core of Autism," Interactive Autism Network, January 16, 2009. www.iancommu nity.org/cs/what_do_we_know/social_skills_interventions.

34. Exkorn, *The Autism Sourcebook*, pp. 84–85.

35. Interdisciplinary Council on Developmental and Learning Disorders (ICDL), "What's DIR/Floortime?" www.icdl.com/ dirFloortime/overview/index.shtml.

36. ICDL, "Six Developmental Stages." www.icdl.com/dirFloor time/overview/SixDevelopmentalMilestones.shtml.
37. ICDL, "Six Developmental Stages."
38. ICDL, "Six Developmental Stages."
39. ICDL, "Six Developmental Stages."
40. ICDL, "Six Developmental Stages."
41. Jenny McCarthy, *Mother Warriors*. New York: Dutton, 2008, p. 52.
42. McCarthy, *Mother Warriors*, p. 10.
43. Quoted in National Advisory Committee on Immunization, "Thimerosal: Updated Statement," *Canada Communicable Disease Report*, vol. 33, July 1, 2007, reprinted at Autism Watch. www.autism-watch.org/news/thimerosal_canada .shtml.

Chapter Five: Living with an ASD

44. Williams, *Nobody Nowhere*, pp. 67, 68.
45. Williams, *Nobody Nowhere*, pp. 68–69.
46. Grandin, *Thinking in Pictures*, p. 62.
47. Grandin and Johnson, *Animals in Translation*, pp. 4–5.
48. Grandin, *Thinking in Pictures*, p. 63.
49. Grandin, *Thinking in Pictures*, p. 63.
50. Grandin, *Thinking in Pictures*, pp. 60–61.
51. Thomas A. McKean, "Seven Things Thomas Wishes He Could Say to You," Thomas A. McKean's Web Site. www .thomasamckean.com/lists/seventhings.htm.
52. Thomas A. McKean, "One Explanation of Sensory Overload," Thomas A. McKean's Web Site. www.thomasamc kean.com/gallery/albums/writings/Overload.pdf.
53. McKean, "One Explanation of Sensory Overload."
54. McKean, "Seven Things Thomas Wishes He Could Say to You."
55. Kamran Nazeer, *Send in the Idiots: Stories from the Other Side of Autism*. New York: Bloomsbury, 2006, p. 143.
56. Sue Rubin, "Autism Is a World," DVD recording, directed and produced by Gerardine Wurzburg. CNN Presents and State of the Art, Inc., 2004.
57. Karasik and Karasik, *The Ride Together*, p. 181.
58. Karasik and Karasik, *The Ride Together*, pp. 182, 185.

Chapter Six: The Search for a Cure

59. Autism Speaks.org, "Our Mission." www.autismspeaks.org /goals.php.

60. David G. Amaral, "Welcome to the Autism Phenome Project!" UC Davis M.I.N.D. Institute. www.ucdmc.ucdavis .edu/mindinstitute/research/app/amaralwelcome.html.

61. Quoted in Karen Finney, "Autism Experts to Be Featured on CBS," UC Newsroom, February 15, 2007. www.university ofcalifornia.edu/news/article/8923.

62. Quoted in Phyllis Brown, "Unusual Use of Toys in Infancy a Clue to Later Autism," Eureka Alert, UC Davis-Health System, November 6, 2008. www.eurekalert.org/pub_releases/ 2008-11/uoc—uuo110608.php.

63. *ScienceDaily*, "Drug Reverses Mental Retardation Caused by Genetic Disorder; Hope for Correcting How Autism Disrupts Brain," University of California–Los Angeles, June 23, 2008. www.sciencedaily.com/releases/2008/06/0806222244 28.htm.

64. Susan Hyman, "Diet and Behavior in Young Children with Autism," STAART Network Centers: University of Rochester, National Institute of Mental Health. www.nimh.nih.gov/ research-funding/scientific-meetings/recurring-meetings/iacc /nih-initiatives/staart/staart-network-centers-university-of- rochester.shtml.

65. Autism Speaks.org, "Treatment Initiative." www.autism speaks.org/science/research/initiatives/treatment_initiative .php.

66. Autistics.org: Home. http://autistics.org.

67. Jim Sinclair, "Don't Mourn for Us," Autism Information Library, Autistics.org. www.autistics.org/library/dontmourn.html.

68. Amanda Baggs, "Love, Devotion, Hope, Prevention, and Cure," Autism Information Library, Autistics.org. www .autistics.org/library/love.html.

69. Nazeer, *Send in the Idiots*, p. 216.

70. Exkorn, *The Autism Sourcebook*, p. 170.

Glossary

applied behavior analysis (ABA): A scientifically designed treatment method that uses a system of rewards to teach specific behaviors and skills and to reduce unwanted behaviors.

brain plasticity: The ability of the brain to rewire and change its organization because of learning experiences, especially in the first few years of life.

clinicians: Professionals, such as psychiatrists, psychologists, and medical doctors, who provide diagnosis, treatment, and therapy to patients and clients.

corpus callosum: The nerve tissue that connects the two hemispheres of the brain and allows them to communicate with each other.

deoxyribonucleic acid (DNA): The chemicals in the genes that carry the coding instructions for all the body's structures and functions.

DIR/Floortime: A treatment method that emphasizes emotional relationships and engaging a child's interests at his or her level of ability while socially interacting intensely with the child.

echolalia: The repetition or parroting of words or phrases spoken by others.

gene: A discrete segment of DNA on a specific point of a chromosome that carries a specific unit of inheritance.

neurological: Involving the nervous system—the brain, spinal cord, and nerves.

nonverbal: Having no communication in words; without spoken language.

obsessive: Excessive, persistent, and uncontrollable; often interfering with other activities.

prognosis: Predicted outcome.

stereotyped: Purposeless and repetitive but performed in exactly the same way over and over.

toxin: A poisonous substance that can cause disease or harm.

vaccines: Injections, or shots, administered to protect against diseases such as measles, polio, or whooping cough.

Organizations to Contact

Association for Science in Autism Treatment (ASAT)
PO Box 188
Crosswicks, NJ 08515
e-mail: info@asatonline.org
Web site: www.asatonline.org

ASAT is dedicated to improving the education, care, and treatment of people with autism. It is especially concerned with identifying questionable treatments and cures and helping families get scientifically supported, accurate information.

Autism Information Center
Centers for Disease Control and Prevention (CDC)
1600 Clifton Rd.
Atlanta, GA 30333
phone: (800) 232-4636
e-mail: cdcinfo@cdc.gov
Web site: www.cdc.gov

At this government Web site, visitors can find information about autism spectrum disorders, downloadable fact sheets, and general publications. The CDC's Autism Information Center conducts and funds research into all aspects of autism spectrum disorders.

Autism Society of America (ASA)
7910 Woodmont Ave., Ste. 300
Bethesda, MD 20814
phone: (800) 328-8476
Web site: www.autism-society.org

ASA is a national organization founded by psychologist Bernard Rimland and advocating the theory that autism is a neurological disorder caused by genetic sensitivity to environmental toxins and vaccines that lead to brain abnormalities.

The society is dedicated to improving the lives of autistic people and providing information to parents and families.

Autism Speaks
2 Park Ave., 11th Fl.
New York, NY 10016
phone: (212) 252-8584
e-mail: contactus@autismspeaks.org
Web site: www.autismspeaks.org

Autism Speaks is an activist advocacy organization supporting scientific research into the causes, treatments, prevention, and cure of autism. It also supports families with autistic members through an interactive online community.

Generation Rescue
phone: (877) 98AUTISM (982-8847)
e-mail: info2@generationrescue.org
Web site: www.generationrescue.org

This Web site is Jenny McCarthy's parent-to-parent autism organization devoted to fighting for research into the harm vaccines do to children and to advocating medical treatments to heal autistic children.

For Further Reading

Books

Fiona Bleach, *Everybody Is Different: A Book for Young People Who Have Brothers or Sisters with Autism.* Shawnee Mission, KS: Autism Asperger, 2002. This nontechnical, simply written book answers many questions that young people may have about an autistic sibling.

Temple Grandin and Kate Duffy, *Developing Talents: Careers for Individuals with Asperger Syndrome and High-Functioning Autism.* Shawnee Mission, KS: Autism Asperger, 2004. Grandin and her coauthor (who is the mother of two autistic teens) use their personal experiences to give practical advice to teens on the autism spectrum. Among other topics, they discuss how to turn special talents and interests into careers, how to search for a job, and how to cope with sensory issues in the workplace.

Luke Jackson, *Freaks, Geeks, and Asperger Syndrome: A User Guide to Adolescence.* London: Jessica Kingsley, 2002. The author has the mildest form of autism spectrum disorder and also has a sibling with autistic disorder. He wrote this book of advice for teens when he was thirteen years old. The book not only showcases his humor and intelligence but also provides insight into living with an ASD.

Peggy J. Parks, *Compact Research: Autism.* San Diego: ReferencePoint, 2008. Read about the major theories on the cause, prevention, and treatment of autism spectrum disorders. Compare different viewpoints and conflicting opinions and explore the issue of the effectiveness of today's treatments.

Ana Maria Rodriguez, *Autism and Asperger Syndrome.* Minneapolis: Twenty-First Century, 2009. This book includes many fascinating accounts of young people with autism spectrum disorders, along with the latest information on causes, diagnoses, and treatments.

Web Sites

Donna Williams: Front Page (www.donnawilliams.net). Williams discusses her autism and the effect it has had on her life, shares her art and poetry, and maintains a blog where she writes about her opinions on just about anything.

HowStuffWorks: "Can TV Viewing Cause Autism?" (http://health.howstuffworks.com/tv-autism.htm). This interesting article by Julia Layton discusses research that suggests autism can be triggered by living where it rains a lot and by watching too much television.

Neuroscience for Kids (http://faculty.washington.edu/chudler/introb.html). At this site from the University of Washington, visitors can learn all about the brain, its lobes, and its wiring. The site has illustrations of the parts of the brain, too. Click on the link for autism to learn more about its effects on the brain.

TeensHealth: Autism (http://kidshealth.org/teen/diseases_conditions/learning/autism.html). This short article gives an overview of autism and discusses what teens with autism may be like.

Temple Grandin.com (www.templegrandin.com/templehome.html). Visitors to Professor Grandin's Web site can learn about her contributions and discoveries in the field of animal behavior, as well as explore her ideas about autism. Click on the link for the Squeeze Machine to see blueprints for its construction, and click the link for the complete paper about deep touch pressure to see a photograph of the Squeeze Machine.

WrongPlanet.net (www.wrongplanet.net). This site is a Web community for anyone with an autism spectrum disorder. It offers support, news, information, opinions, and community forums where people can interact with others on the autism spectrum. In general, the members are strong opponents of curing or preventing ASDs.

YouTube: Autism Is a World—Open (www.youtube.com/watch?v=U1wsiVYCqn0). Watch a short video of Sue Rubin, a young woman with autism, as she moves through her day.

Index

Picture Credits

About the Author

Toney Allman holds a bachelor of science degree in psychology from Ohio State University and a master's degree in clinical psychology from the University of Hawaii. She currently lives in rural Virginia and has written more than thirty nonfiction books for students. She remembers when autism was considered a rare disorder and behavioral treatment methods were in their infancy.